Number in Preschool and Kindergarten: Educational Implications of Piaget's Theory

by
Constance Kamii
University of Illinois at Chicago Circle
and
University of Geneva (Switzerland)

National Association for the
Education of Young Children
Washington, D.C.

Photographs: Constance Kamii and Rheta DeVries
Cover design: Melanie White
Book design: Rebecca Miller

Copyright © 1982 Constance Kamii. Second printing 1984, third printing 1986, fourth printing 1988, fifth printing 1990.

The National Association for the Education of Young Children attempts through its publications program to provide a forum for discussion of major issues and ideas in our field. We hope to provoke thought and promote professional growth. The views expressed or implied are not necessarily those of the Association.

Library of Congress Catalog Card Number: 82-81943
ISBN Catalog Number: 0-912674-80-6
NAEYC #103
Printed in the United States of America.

This book is also available in Japanese from Child Honsha, Tokyo; in Spanish from Visor Libros, Roble, 22, Madrid-20, Spain; and in Portugese from Papirus Livros, Rua Sacramento, 202, CEP 13 100-CAMPINAS-SP Brazil.

Contents

Acknowledgments

This book was written to correct the errors and inadequacies in *Piaget, Children, and Number* (Kamii and DeVries 1976). I am grateful to Marianne Denis-Prinzhorn (University of Geneva), Eleanor Duckworth (Harvard University), and Mary Barg and Mary Kay Willert (former students at the University of Illinois at Chicago Circle) for giving me their critical reactions to the 1976 version. I would also like to express appreciation to Hermina Sinclair (University of Geneva) for contributing many of the ideas presented in this book, and to Kathleen Gruber and Diann El-Nahal (University of Illinois at Chicago Circle), Lucinda Lee-Katz (Erikson Institute for Early Education), and Ed Labinowicz (California State University at Northridge) for critically reading the manuscript and offering many valuable suggestions.

The assistance of Patricia Chronis, Director; Maureen Ellis, Assistant Director; and the teachers of Circle Children's Center (University of Illinois at Chicago Circle) is also gratefully acknowledged.

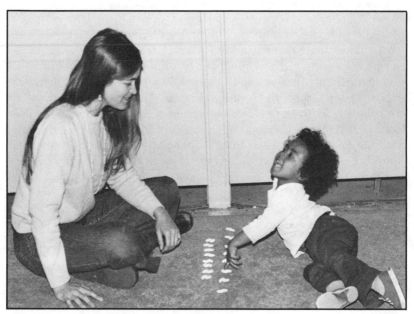

Photograph 1. *The conservation of number task.*

Introduction

Many four-year-olds can put out as many Styrofoam pieces as the eight that the teacher has put out in a row. When their set is spread out as shown in Photograph 1, however, many of them believe that they now have more than the teacher.

When educators hear about this phenomenon of nonconservation, they inevitably wonder what it means for teaching number in the classroom. Some conclude that nonconservers must be taught to conserve number.[1] Lavatelli (1973), for example, suggested that the teacher remind the child of one-to-one correspondence by making a bridge (see Figure 1) with a pipe cleaner connecting each element of one set with the corresponding element of the other set. Such direct teaching of the conservation task is a misapplication of Piaget's research.[2] When I thus criticize such attempts to apply Piaget's research in the classroom, I am asked, "How, then, do you propose to teach number?"

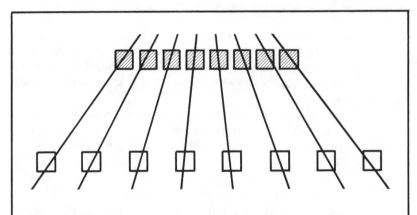

Figure 1. *An attempt to teach children to conserve by making bridges to show one-to-one correspondence.*

---

[1]*To conserve number* means to think that the quantity remains the same when the spatial arrangement of the objects has been changed. This statement will be clarified shortly in the description of the conservation of number task.

[2]This approach is like trying to make children more intelligent by teaching correct answers to the Binet test, as it teaches children to give correct answers to the specific questions asked in the conservation task without enabling them to construct the underlying logico-mathematical structure of number. This statement will be clarified later.

"Isn't there any way to apply this theory in the classroom?"

The purpose of this book is to answer these questions. Piaget's research and theory are indeed useful to the classroom teacher, and can make a major difference in how we teach elementary number. I will focus on how the teacher can use the theory in a practical way by discussing the following four topics:

1. The nature of number
2. Objectives for "teaching" number
3. Principles of teaching
4. Situations in school that the teacher can use to "teach" number

For readers unfamiliar with the conservation of elementary number task, I would like to review it briefly (Inhelder, Sinclair, and Bovet 1974, pp. 275–277).

A. Method[3]
   Materials: 20 red counters
              20 blue counters

   Procedure
   1. Equality
      The experimenter lays out one row of about 8 blue counters (at least 7)[4] and asks the child to put out the same number of red ones, saying, "Put out as many of your red counters as I've put blue ones . . . (exactly the same number, just as many, no more, no less)."

      The child's response is recorded in his protocol. If necessary, the experimenter then puts the red and blue counters in one-to-one correspondence and asks the child whether or not the two rows have the same amount.
   2. Conservation
      The experimenter modifies the layout in front of the child's watchful eyes by spacing out the counters in one of the rows, or by moving them together (see Figure 2). The following questions are then asked: "Are there as many (the same number of) blue

---

[3]From the description which follows, the interviews might appear rather standardized. Each interview must be adapted to the particular subject, especially with regard to the latter's understanding of the terms used in quantification.

[4]Piaget referred to small numbers up to four or five as *perceptual numbers* because small numbers such as "oo" and "ooo" can easily be distinguished at a glance, perceptually. When seven objects are presented, however, it is impossible to distinguish "ooooooo" from "oooooooo," for example, by perception alone.

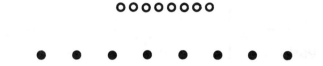

Figure 2. *The arrangement of the objects when the child is asked if there are as many blue ones as red ones, or more blue ones, or more red ones.*

ones as red ones, or are there more here (blue) or more here (red)? How do you know?"

3. Countersuggestion
   a. If the child has given a correct conservation answer, the experimenter says, "Look how long this line is. Another child said there are more counters in it because this row is longer. Who is right, you or the other child?"
   b. If the child's answer was wrong, however, the experimenter reminds him of the initial equality: "But don't you remember, before, we put one red counter in front of each blue one. Another child said that there is the same number of red and blue ones now. Who do you think is right, you or the other child?"
4. Quotity[5]

   The experimenter asks the child to count the blue ones, and when the child has finished counting them, the experimenter hides the red ones and asks, "How many red ones do you think there are? Can you guess without counting them? How do you know?"

B. Levels

Table 1 summarizes the hierarchical order of development. At level I, the child cannot make a set that has the same number. Needless to say, therefore, he cannot conserve the equality of the two sets either. Some of these children put out all the red counters haphazardly as shown in Figure 3(a). They stop putting out counters only because there are no

---

[5]Quotity (*quotité* in French as opposed to *quantité*, that means *quantity*) refers to the result of counting. After counting eight objects in the blue row, some nonconservers can guess that there must be eight in the red row. These children nevertheless often continue to believe that there are more in the row that is longer.

	Equality	Conservation
Level I	−	−
Level II	+	−
Level III	+	+

Table 1. *The hierarchical order of development in the conservation of elementary number.*

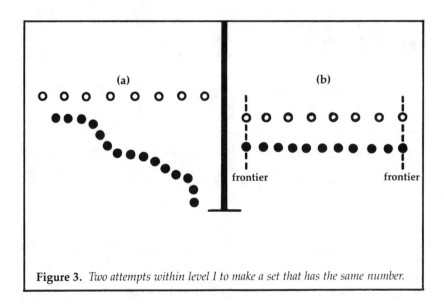

Figure 3. *Two attempts within level I to make a set that has the same number.*

more left to put out. Figure 3(b) shows a more advanced response within level I. The children who do this do not put the same number out but carefully use the spatial frontiers of the rows as the criterion for deciding the "sameness" of the two quantities. (When they have not yet built the beginning of the mental structure of number shown in Figure 5(b), children use the best criterion they can think of, that in this case is the spatial frontiers of the two sets.)

At level II, that is found up to four to five years of age, the child can make a set that has the same number but cannot conserve this equality.[6] When he is asked the conservation question, he says, for example, "There are more red ones because the blue ones are all squashed together."

Level III children are conservers. They give correct answers to all the questions, are not swayed by countersuggestions, and give one or more of the following arguments to explain why they think the two rows have the same quantity:

a. "There are just as many blue ones as red ones because it was the same much before, and we haven't taken anything away, they've just been squashed up" (the *identity* argument).

b. "We could put all the red ones back the way they were before, so there aren't more blue ones or red ones" (the *reversibility* argument).

c. "Here the red ones are in a long row, but there's space in between the counters, so that makes it the same" (the *compensation* argument).

Conservation is not achieved overnight, and between levels II and III is an intermediate level. Intermediate level children give the correct answer to only one of the questions when one row is made longer and the other row is subsequently made longer, or they hesitate and/or keep changing their minds ("There are more blue ones . . . no, red ones . . . they're both the same . . ."). Even when these children give correct answers, they cannot justify them adequately.

The quotity question shows that the relationship between language and thought is not simple. Some level II children give the correct answer ("There are eight blue ones; so I think there are eight red ones as well.") but think there are more in one row than in the other. At the intermediate level, however, children always give the correct answer to the quotity question.

When educators first find out about the above levels, they often

---

[6]The ages mentioned are approximate. These vary with the cultural and educational setting of the subject.

think that their job is to get children to the next developmental level. In the following section on the nature of number, I will try to show that this is a misapplication of Piaget's theory. According to him, number is constructed by each child out of all kinds of relationships that he creates among objects. I hope the discussion will also clarify why I stated earlier that the direct teaching of conservation is a misapplication of Piaget's theory.

1
The nature of number

Piaget made a fundamental distinction among three kinds of knowledge according to their ultimate sources and mode of structuring: physical knowledge, logico-mathematical knowledge, and social (conventional) knowledge. Number is an example of logico-mathematical knowledge. I will discuss below the logico-mathematical nature of number, first in contrast with physical knowledge and then with social (conventional) knowledge.

Logico-mathematical and physical knowledge

Piaget conceptualized two types, or poles, of knowledge—physical knowledge at one end and logico-mathematical knowledge at the other. Physical knowledge is knowledge of objects in external reality. The color and weight of a chip are examples of physical properties that are *in* objects in external reality, and can be known by observation. The knowledge that a chip will fall when we let go of it in the air is also an example of physical knowledge.

When, however, we are presented with a red chip and a blue one, and note that they are different, this difference is an example of logico-mathematical knowledge. The chips are indeed observable, but the difference between them is not. The difference is a *relationship* created mentally by the individual who puts the two objects into a relationship. The difference is neither *in* one chip nor *in* the other, and if a person did not put the objects into this relationship, the difference would not exist for him.

Other examples of relationships the individual can create between the two chips are *similar, the same in weight*, and *two*. It is just as correct to say that the red and blue chips are similar as it is to say that they are different. The relationship an individual puts the objects into is up to that individual. From one point of view the two chips are different, and from another point of view they are similar. If the individual wants to compare the weight of the two chips, he is likely to say that the objects are "the same" (in weight). If, however, he wants to view the objects numerically, he will say that there are "two." The two chips are observable, but the "two-ness" is not. Number is a relationship created mentally by each individual.[7]

The child goes on to construct logico-mathematical knowledge by coordinating the simple relationships he created between objects earlier. Logico-mathematical knowledge consists of the coordination of relationships. For example, by coordinating the relationships of *same*, *different*, and *more*, the child becomes able to deduce that there are more beads in the world than red beads, and that there are more animals than cows. It is likewise by coordinating the relationship between "two" and "two" that he comes to deduce that $2 + 2 = 4$, and that $2 \times 2 = 4$.

Piaget thus recognized external and internal sources of knowledge. The source of physical knowledge (as well as social knowledge) is partly[8] external to the individual. The source of logico-mathematical knowledge, by contrast, is internal. This statement will be clarified by the following discussion of two kinds of abstraction through which the child constructs physical and logico-mathematical knowledge.

The construction of logico-mathematical and physical knowledge: empirical and reflective abstraction

Piaget's view about the logico-mathematical nature of number is in sharp contrast with the math educators' view that is found in most

---

[7]I hasten to say that "two" is not a good number to choose to illustrate the logico-mathematical nature of number. Piaget makes a distinction between *perceptual numbers* and *numbers*. Perceptual numbers are small numbers up to four or five that can be distinguished by perception, without requiring logico-mathematical structuring. Even some birds can be trained to discriminate between "oo" and "ooo". However, the distinction between "ooooooo" and "oooooooo" is impossible by perception alone. Small numbers greater than four or five are called *elementary numbers*. The conservation task described earlier uses seven or eight objects and involves elementary numbers.

Although "two" is a perceptual number, it can also be a logico-mathematical number for an adult who has constructed the entire system of logico-mathematical numbers. I chose the number two in this example in spite of the problem of perceptual numbers because, with 2 counters, I can illustrate other simple relationships such as *different*, *similar*, and *the same in weight*.

[8]My reason for saying *partly* will become clear when I discuss empirical and reflective abstraction.

texts. One typical modern math text (Duncan et al. 1972) states, for example, that number is "a property of sets in the same way that ideas like color, size, and shape refer to properties of objects" (p. T30). Accordingly, children are presented with sets of four pencils, four flowers, four balloons, and five pencils, for example, and are asked to find the sets that have the same "number property." This exercise reflects the assumption that children learn number concepts by abstracting "number properties" from various sets in the same way they abstract color and other physical properties from objects.

In Piaget's theory, the abstraction of color from objects is considered very different in nature from the abstraction of number. The two are so different, in fact, that they are distinguished by different terms. For the abstraction of properties from objects, Piaget used the term *empirical* (or *simple*) abstraction. For the abstraction of number, he used the term *reflective* abstraction.

In empirical abstraction, all the child does is focus on a certain property of the object and ignore the others. For example, when he abstracts the color of an object, the child simply ignores the other properties such as weight and the material with which the object is made (i.e., plastic, wood, metal, etc.).

Reflective abstraction, in contrast, involves the construction of relationships between/among objects. Relationships, as stated earlier, do not have an existence in external reality. The difference between one chip and another does not exist *in* one chip or the other, nor anywhere else in external reality. This relationship exists only in the minds of those who can create it between the objects. The term *constructive* abstraction might be easier to understand than *reflective* abstraction to indicate that this abstraction is a construction by the mind rather than a focus on something that already exists in objects.

Having made the distinction between empirical and reflective abstraction, Piaget went on to say that, in the psychological reality of the young child, one cannot take place without the other. For example, the child could not construct the relationship *different* if he could not observe different properties in objects. Likewise, the relationship *two* would be impossible to construct if the child thought that objects behave like drops of water (that can combine to become one drop). Conversely, the child could not construct physical knowledge if he did not have a logico-mathematical framework that enables him to put new observations into relationship with the knowledge he already has. To note that a certain fish is red, for example, the child needs a classificatory scheme to distinguish *red* from *all other colors*. He also needs a classificatory scheme to distinguish *fish* from all the other kinds of objects he already knows. A logico-mathematical framework (constructed by reflective abstraction) is thus necessary for empirical abstraction because no fact could be "read" from external reality if each fact were an isolated bit of knowledge without any relationship to the knowledge already built in an organized fashion.

While reflective abstraction thus cannot take place independently of empirical abstraction during the sensorimotor and preoperational periods, it later becomes possible for reflective abstraction to take place independently. For example, once the child has constructed number (by reflective abstraction), he will become able to operate on numbers and do 5 + 5 and 5 × 2 (by reflective abstraction). The fact that reflective abstraction cannot occur independently before the child's construction of earlier relationships has important implications for the teaching of number. It implies that the child must put all kinds of content (objects, events, and actions) into all kinds of relationships if he is to construct number. This principle will be elaborated shortly below and in Chapter 3, on principles of teaching.

The distinction between the two kinds of abstraction may seem unimportant while the child is learning small numbers, say, up to 10. When he goes on to larger numbers such as 999 and 1000, however, it becomes clear that it is impossible to learn every number all the way to infinity by empirical abstraction from sets of objects or pictures! Numbers are learned not by empirical abstraction from sets that are already made but by reflective abstraction as the child constructs relationships. Because these relationships are created by the mind, it is possible to understand numbers such as 1,000,002 even if we have never seen or counted 1,000,002 objects in a set.

The construction of number: the synthesis of order and hierarchical inclusion

Number according to Piaget is a synthesis of two kinds of relationships the child creates among objects (by reflective abstraction). One is order, and the other is hierarchical inclusion.

I would like to begin by discussing what Piaget meant by order. All teachers of young children have seen the common tendency among children to count objects by skipping some and counting some more than once. When given eight objects, for example, a child who can recite "One, two, three, four . . . " correctly up to ten may end up claiming that there are ten things by counting as shown in Figure 4(a). This tendency shows that the child does not feel the logical necessity of putting the objects in an order to make sure he does not skip any or count the same one more than once. The only way we can be sure of not overlooking any or counting the same object more than once is by putting them in an order. The child, however, does not have to put the objects literally in a spatial order to put them into an ordered relationship. What is important is that he order them mentally as shown in Figure 4(b).

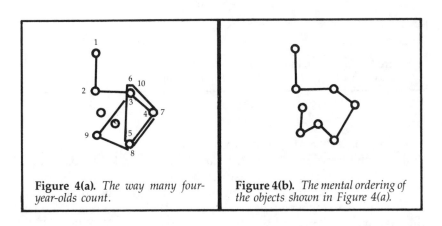

Figure 4(a). *The way many four-year-olds count.*

Figure 4(b). *The mental ordering of the objects shown in Figure 4(a).*

If ordering were the only mental action on objects, the objects would not be quantified, since the child could consider them one at a time rather than a group of many at the same time. For example, after counting eight objects arranged in an ordered relationship as shown in Figure 5(a), the child usually states that there are eight. If we then ask him to show us the eight, he sometimes points to the last one (the eighth object). This behavior indicates that, for this child, the words *one, two, three,* etc. are names for individual elements in the series, like *John, Marie, Suzy,* . . . *Peter.* When asked how many there are, therefore, the child says what amounts to *Peter.* The name *Peter* stands for the last individual in the series and not for the entire group. To quantify the objects as a group, the child has to put them in a relationship of hierarchical inclusion. This relationship, shown in Figure 5(b), means that the child mentally includes *one* in *two, two* in *three, three* in *four,* etc. When presented with eight objects, he can quantify the set numerically only if he can put all the objects into a single relationship syn-

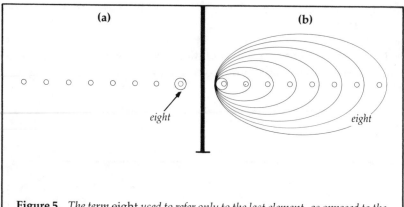

Figure 5. *The term* eight *used to refer only to the last element, as opposed to the same word used with the structure of hierarchical inclusion.*

thesizing[9] order[10] and hierarchical inclusion.

Young children's reaction to the class-inclusion task[11] helps us understand how difficult it is to construct the hierarchical structure. In the class-inclusion task, the child is given six miniature dogs and two cats of the same size, for example, and is asked, "What do you see?" so that the examiner can proceed with whatever word came from the child's vocabulary. The child is then asked to show *"all* the animals," *"all* the dogs," and *"all* the cats" with the words that the child used (e.g., *doggy*).

[9]Another term for *synthesis* is the *reciprocal assimilation of two schemes*—the scheme of ordering, and that of hierarchically including one in two, two in three, etc.

[10]While it is necessary to order the objects to make sure that none is skipped or counted more than once, the specific order becomes irrelevant once an object has been counted. Once it has been counted, the object becomes included in the category of those already counted, just like any other object, and it does not matter whether the particular object was the third, fourth, or fifth object in the order.

[11]The class-inclusion task aims at determining the child's ability to coordinate the quantitative and qualitative aspects of a class and a subclass. For example, the child who says that there are more dogs than animals is not coordinating the quantitative and qualitative aspects of the class (animals) and a subclass (dogs).

Class inclusion is similar to the hierarchical structure of number but different. Class inclusion deals with qualities such as those that characterize dogs, cats, and animals. In number, however, all qualities are irrelevant, as a dog and a cat are both considered to be "ones." Another difference between number and class inclusion is that, in number, there is only one element at each hierarchical level. In a class, there is usually more than one element.

Only after ascertaining the child's understanding of these words does the adult ask the following class-inclusion question: "Are there more dogs or more animals?"

Four-year-olds typically answer, "More dogs," whereupon the adult asks, "Than what?" The four-year-old's answer is "Than cats." In other words, the question the examiner asks is "Are there more dogs or more animals?" but what young children "hear" is "Are there more dogs or more cats?" Young children hear a question that is different from the one the adult asked because once they have mentally cut the whole (animals) into two parts (cats and dogs), the only thing they can think about is the two parts. For them, at that moment, the whole no longer exists. They can think about the whole, but not when they are thinking about the parts. In order to compare the whole with a part, the child has to do two opposite mental actions at the same time—cut the whole into two parts and put the parts back together into a whole. This, according to Piaget, is precisely what four-year-olds cannot do.

By seven to eight years of age, most children's thought becomes mobile enough to be reversible. Reversibility refers to the ability to mentally do opposite actions simultaneously—in this case, to cut the whole into two parts and reunite the parts into a whole. In physical, material action it is not possible to do two opposite things simultaneously. In our heads, however, this is possible when thought has become mobile enough to be reversible. It is only when the parts can be reunited in the mind that a child can "see" that there are more animals than dogs.

Piaget thus explained the attainment of the hierarchical structure of class inclusion by the increasing mobility of children's thought. This is why it is important for children to put all kinds of content (objects, events, and actions) into all kinds of relationships. When children put all kinds of content into relationships, their thought becomes more mobile, and one of the results of this mobility is the logico-mathematical structure of number shown in Figure 5(b).

Logico-mathematical and social (conventional) knowledge

Piaget's theory of number is also in contrast with the common assumption that number concepts can be taught by social transmission like social (conventional) knowledge, especially by teaching children how to count. Examples of social (conventional) knowledge are the facts that Christmas comes on December 25, that a tree is called *tree*, that some people shake hands under certain circumstances, and that tables are not to stand on. The ultimate source of social knowledge is conventions worked out by people. The main characteristic of social knowledge is that it is largely arbitrary in nature. The fact that some people celebrate Christmas while others do not is an example of the arbitrariness of social knowledge. There is no physical or logical reason for December 25 to be considered any different from any other day of the year. The fact that a tree is called *tree* is likewise completely arbitrary. In another language, the same object is called by another name since there is no physical or logical relationship between an object and its name. It follows that, for the child's acquisition of social knowledge, input from people is indispensable.

The preceding statement does not imply that input from people is all that the child needs to acquire social knowledge. Like physical knowledge, social knowledge is knowledge of content and requires a logico-mathematical framework for its assimilation and organization. Just as the child needs a logico-mathematical framework to recognize a red fish as such (physical knowledge), he needs the same logico-mathematical framework to recognize an obscene word as such (social knowledge). To recognize an obscene word, the child needs to make dichotomies between "obscene words" and "words that are not obscene" and between "words" and "everything else." The same logico-mathematical framework is used by the child to construct both physical and social knowledge.

People who believe that number concepts should be taught by social transmission fail to make the fundamental distinction between logico-mathematical and social knowledge. In logico-mathematical knowledge, the ultimate source of knowledge is the child himself, and absolutely nothing is arbitrary in this domain. For example, 2 + 3 gives the same result in all cultures. In fact, every culture that builds any mathematics at all ends up building exactly the same mathematics, as this is a system of relationships in which absolutely nothing is arbitrary. To cite another example of the universality and nonarbitrary nature of logico-mathematical knowledge, there are more animals than cows in all cultures.

The words *one, two, three, four* are examples of social knowledge. Each language has a different set of words for counting. But the underlying idea of number belongs to logico-mathematical knowledge, which is universal.

Piaget's view is thus in contrast with the belief that there is a "world of numbers" into which each child must be socialized. To be sure, there is consensus about the sum of 2 + 3, but neither number nor addition is "out there" in the social world, to be transmitted from people. Children can be taught to give the correct answer to 2 + 3, but they cannot be taught directly the relationships underlying this addition. Likewise, even two-year-olds can see the difference between a pile of three blocks and a pile of ten blocks. But this does not imply that number is "out there" in the physical world, to be learned by empirical abstraction.

The implication of the conservation task for educators

For educators, the significance of the conservation task lies mainly in epistemology. Epistemology is the study of knowledge that addresses questions such as "What is the nature of number?" and "How did people come to know number?" Piaget invented the conservation task to answer these kinds of questions. With this task, he proved that number is not something that is known innately by intuition or empirically by observation. The fact that young children do not conserve number before five years of age shows that number is not innately known and takes many years to construct. If it were knowable by observation, it would be enough for children younger than five to see the one-to-one correspondence between the two rows to know that the two sets in Figure 2 have the same quantity. Piaget also proved with the conservation task that number concepts are not acquired through language. If they were, children would not say that there are eight in each row, but the longer row has more.[12]

With this task and many others, Piaget and his collaborators showed that number is something that each human being constructs by creating and coordinating relationships. Because number is constructed by each individual, we see the sequence of development summarized in Table 1. At level I, the child cannot even make a set that has the same number. At level II, he becomes able to do this because he has begun to

---

[12]The quotity task (Gréco 1962) shows, however, that counting can sometimes be a useful tool for thinking. After getting a nonconserving answer from the child, Gréco sometimes obtained a conserving answer by asking the child to count the two rows. Gréco and Piaget's interpretation of this phenomenon is that when the child is at a higher, transitional level, language can be a useful tool that sometimes enables him to think at an even higher level.

construct the logico-mathematical (mental) structure of number shown in Figure 5(b). However, this emerging structure is not strong enough yet to enable him to conserve the numerical equality of the two sets. By level III, he has constructed a numerical structure that has become powerful enough to enable him to view the objects numerically, rather than spatially.

Note that when the child does not yet have the (mental) structure of number at levels I and II, he bases his judgment on space, or the perception of the frontiers. At level I, as can be seen in Figure 3(b), he uses the frontiers of the rows to make a set that has "the same amount." At level II, when one row goes beyond the frontiers of the other as shown in Figure 2, the child concludes that this row has "more." A child who does not have the (mental) structure of number uses the best thing he can think of to make quantitative judgments, namely space. When he has constructed the structure of number, however, the space occupied by the objects becomes irrelevant, as the child makes quantitative judgments by imposing a numerical structure on the objects.

While the conservation task was conceived to answer epistemological questions, it can also be used to answer psychological questions concerning where individual children are in the developmental sequence. For educators, however, it is absurd to train children to give higher-level answers on this task. The reason is that performance on this task is one thing, and the development of the underlying mental structure illustrated in Figure 5(b) is quite another thing. Educators must foster the development of this structure, rather than trying to teach children to give correct surface answers on the conservation task.

Findings from another task may clarify the difference between performance on a task and the underlying mental structure. I will discuss briefly below the highlights of a task called *connexity* conducted by Morf (1962) in collaboration with Piaget. We will see that although the mental structure of number becomes formed well enough by age five to six to enable the majority of children to conserve elementary number, it is not structured sufficiently before seven-and-one-half years of age to permit him to know that all consecutive numbers are connected by the operation of " + 1." In the connexity task, Morf presented the child with 9 cubes (2 cm^3 in size) shown as A in Figure 6(a). He put about 30 other cubes on a ruler in a line, and dropped one at a time to begin the linear arrangement marked B. After ascertaining the child's understanding that B could be increased by continuing to drop blocks from the ruler, he put the following question to him: "If I continue to drop the blocks one by one, will I get to exactly the same number here (B) as here (A)?"

At seven-and-one-half years of age, children thought the answer was so obvious that the question was stupid. Before this age, however, they were not sure.

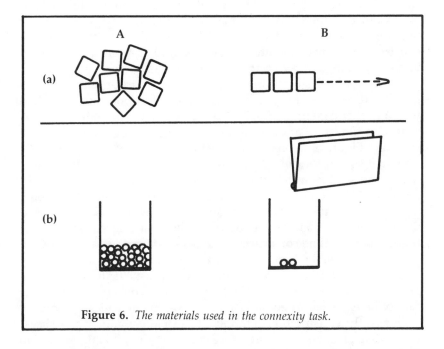

Figure 6. *The materials used in the connexity task.*

When the adult went on to drop one block at a time and asked after each additional block whether the two groups now had the same number, many children kept saying, "No," until they suddenly declared that B had too many. When asked if there was a moment when the two quantities were exactly the same, the children replied, "No, for a long time B did not have enough, but suddenly it had too many."[13] For these children, it was possible to go directly from "not enough" to "too many" without going through "exactly the same number." Others said it was impossible to compare the two quantities because A was a

---

[13]This is exactly what the situation was *for the child*. When the child does not yet have the logico-mathematical structure of number in his head, he uses the best means he has—his eyes. With his eyes, the child observed that B suddenly had more than A. Children who have constructed the structure of number in their heads observe something else because they can interpret the sensory information numerically with the repeated operation of "+1."

heap and B was a line. Still others spoke of the necessity of counting the blocks. This was a rather sophisticated answer but one that masked the absence of logical certitude. By asking the child if counting was the only way of knowing the possibility of getting to the same number, Morf found out that the child often talked about this practical procedure because he could not make a logical deduction. To children who had constructed the logico-mathematical structure of number, the answer was so obvious that counting was superfluous.

The task became slightly more difficult when a large number of small glass beads was used (3 mm^3 in diameter). Morf presented the child with a beaker containing 50–70 of these beads. He then dropped one bead at a time into another beaker from a piece of paper folded as shown in Figure 6(b). Not before seven-and-one-half to eight years of age did it become obvious to children that there had to be a time when the two quantities were exactly the same.

The child becomes able to deduce the logical necessity of going through "the same number" in the above task when he has constructed the logico-mathematical structure of number that enables him to make this deduction. If he constructs the logico-mathematical structure in a solid way, he will become able to reason logically in a wide variety of tasks that are harder than the conservation task. If, however, he is taught merely to give correct answers on the conservation task, he cannot be expected to go on to higher-level mathematical reasoning.

Finally, the construction of number takes place gradually by "slices" rather than all at once. The first slice goes up to about 7, the second to 8–15, and the third to 15–30 (Piaget and Szeminska 1941, Preface to the 3rd edition). Being able to conserve with 8 objects thus does not mean that the child can necessarily conserve when 30 objects are used. The principle of teaching that can be conceptualized on the basis of this progressive structuring is that, for the construction of large numbers, it is important to foster the development of the same cognitive processes that resulted in the construction of small numbers. If children construct small, elementary numbers by putting all kinds of things into all kinds of relationships, they must engage actively in the same kind of thinking to complete the structuring of the rest of the series.

In conclusion, the logico-mathematical structure of number cannot be taught directly, since the child has to construct it for himself. However, I do not draw the pedagogical implication that the only thing the teacher can do is to sit back and wait. There are certain things the teacher can do to encourage children to think actively (to put things into relationships) thereby stimulating the development of this mental structure. These are discussed in the next two chapters as objectives and principles of teaching derived from Piaget's theory.

Photograph 2. *Pick-Up-Sticks.*

The children are playing Pick-Up Sticks with chopsticks. Each player begins his turn by holding all the sticks in one hand and releasing them so that they will scatter all over the floor. He then tries to pick up as many as possible, one at a time, without making any other stick move. If he makes one move, the turn passes to the next person. The winner is the player who picks up more sticks than anybody else.

Young children modify the rules of the game in excellent ways when the teacher fosters the development of their autonomy. For example, one teacher left the room to make a telephone call. When she returned, she found that each turn consisted of only one attempt to pick up one stick. If a player made a stick move, he had to put back on the floor the one he tried to take. This modification made it possible for the players to be much more active than in the original version of the game.

In this game, children think not only numerically but also spatially. One way to make the spatial relationships more complex is to pick up the sticks with a stick, rather than with fingers.

2

Objectives for "teaching" number[14]

It would be a mistake to draw pedagogical implications of the preceding discussion outside the context of Piaget's theory as a whole. In a book on education, Piaget (1948, Chapter IV) stated that the aim of education must be to develop the child's autonomy, which is indissociably social, moral, and intellectual. Arithmetic, as well as every other subject, must be taught in the context of this broad objective.

Autonomy means being governed by oneself. It is the opposite of heteronomy, which means being governed by somebody else. An extreme example of intellectual autonomy is Copernicus, who invented the heliocentric theory and published it in 1543, when everybody else believed the sun revolved around the earth. The scientists of his day even jeered him off the stage, but he was autonomous enough to state the truth as he saw it. A more commonplace example of intellectual autonomy is my niece, who used to believe in Santa Claus. When she was about six, she surprised her mother one day by asking, "How come Santa Claus uses the same wrapping paper as we do?" Her mother's "explanation" satisfied her for a few minutes, but she soon came up with another question: "How come Santa Claus has the same handwriting as Daddy?" This is an example of intellectual autonomy. The child was governed by herself in spite of parental pressure to believe in Santa Claus. Some first graders honestly believe that 5 + 5 = 10, but others only recite these numbers because they are told to. Autonomy as the aim of education implies that children must not be made to say things they do not honestly believe.

Figure 7 shows the relationship between autonomy as the aim of education and success in school. Schools traditionally teach obedience and "right" answers. They thus unwittingly prevent the development

---

[14]"Teaching" is in quotation marks because number is not directly teachable.

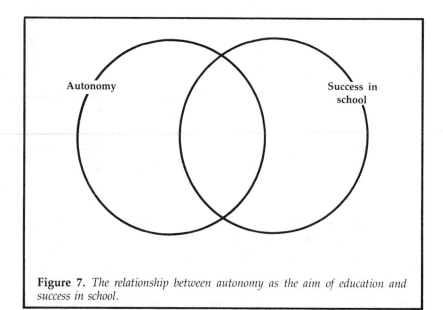

Figure 7. *The relationship between autonomy as the aim of education and success in school.*

of autonomy by reinforcing children's heteronomy. Heteronomy is reinforced by reward and punishment. The way we keep children (and adults) under our control is through the use of these sanctions, and schools make heavy use of grades, teachers' approval, gold stars, citizenship awards, the detention hall, and merits and demerits to get children to be "good." The part of the circle to the right in Figure 7 representing "success in school" that does not overlap with the other circle refers to everything we memorized just to pass one examination after another. Controlled by grades, we memorized words without understanding them or caring about them.

The part of the other circle standing for autonomy that does not overlap with "success in school" includes the ability to think autonomously and critically. Research by McKinnon and Renner (1971) and by Schwebel (1975) shows that college freshmen are not able to think logically enough to be critical and intellectually autonomous. The college students they studied were the "cream of the crop" who were successful enough in school to enter the university. However, the percentage found by McKinnon and Renner to be capable of solid logical thinking at the formal level[15] is 25. The percent found by

---

[15]Formal operations refer to the highest level of logical reasoning in Piaget's theory, that does not appear before adolescence. For more information, see Inhelder and Piaget (1955) and Piaget (1972).

Schwebel is only 20.

After presenting their findings, McKinnon and Renner ask what kind of education these university students received in high school. They go on to say that high schools do not teach students to think logically, and that if high school teachers do not emphasize logical thinking, we must ask who trained these teachers. Their answer is: University professors did. In other words, schools underemphasize critical, autonomous thinking from beginning to end.

The overlap between the two circles in Figure 7 stands for things we learned in school that were useful for our development of autonomy. The ability to read and write, to do arithmetic, to read maps and charts, and to situate events in history are examples of what we learned in school that were useful for our adaptation to the environment. *When autonomy becomes the aim of education, educators will attempt to increase the area of overlap between the two circles.*

Autonomy is indissociably social, moral, and intellectual. An example of autonomy in the social-moral realm is Elliott Richardson, the only person on Nixon's cabinet in the Watergate coverup affair who refused to tell lies and handed in his resignation. Other people on Nixon's staff were examples of the morality of heteronomy, or obedience. When they were told to lie, they obeyed their superior and were governed by the reward system. These people were heteronomous not only morally but also intellectually. A bit of autonomous thinking would have made them realize how stupid it was to expect such lies to go undetected.

A more commonplace example of the indissociability of social, moral, and intellectual autonomy can be found under the first principle of teaching to be discussed shortly, where a boy in a kindergarten class dropped a plateful of salad on the floor. Because Autonomy As the Aim of Education can be found in the Appendix, I will not prolong this discussion. I would like to emphasize, however, that Piaget's theory does not imply just another way of teaching arithmetic. It implies goals that are fundamentally different as shown in Figure 7. It makes an enormous difference when arithmetic, or any other subject, is taught in the context of trying to develop autonomy in children.

Within the context of autonomy as the broad aim of education, I conceptualize the construction of number as the principal objective for arithmetic in preschool and kindergarten. The rest of this book gives many suggestions about the quantification of objects, and it is important to clarify the difference between the construction of number and the quantification of objects. The former (the mental structure shown in Figure 5(b)) exists (or will exist) in the child's head and is, therefore, not observable. The quantification of objects, however, is partly observable. When Andrea tries to take enough cups for everybody at her table, this is an example of the quantification of objects. Part of this quantification is observable in her behavior, but the thinking that takes place in her head is not.

Why do I suggest that the child quantify objects at school? This suggestion is based on the hypothesis that the thinking involved in the child's attempt to quantify objects must help the child construct number, if he is already at a relatively high level of constructing it. Intelligence develops by being used. For example, if an older child does not know how to count money, this is not necessarily a reason for not sending him on an errand to buy a loaf of bread. Having to buy something is often the best way for the child to learn to count money. It is likewise by talking that the child begins to learn how to talk. Although the mental structure is what enables the child to quantify objects, I am hypothesizing that the thinking involved in quantifying objects must also help the child build the mental structure, if he is already at a relatively advanced level of constructing it.

In advocating the child's quantification of objects, I ask teachers to remember that the real objective must not be the observable behavior of quantifying things correctly. The teacher's focus must be on the thinking that takes place in the child's head when she tries to get enough cups for everybody, or two orange sections for each child at the table. It is by thinking that the child constructs the mental structures shown in Figure 5(b).

Findings from research on cross-cultural and socioeconomic status (SES) differences, as well as on urban-rural differences, also suggest what teachers can do in indirect ways to foster the child's construction of number. The research shows that the environment can speed up or retard the development of logico-mathematical knowledge. Children in more industrialized cultures are found generally to develop faster than those in less industrialized cultures. Within the same country, upper-middle-SES children are found to develop faster than lower-SES children, and those living in cities are found to develop faster than those living in rural areas (Adjei 1977; Al-Fakhri 1973; 1977; Al-Shaikh 1974; Almy 1966; 1970; Bovet 1974; Dasen 1972; 1974; De Lacey 1970; De Lemos 1969; Hyde 1970; Laurendeau-Bendavid 1977; Mohseni 1966; Opper 1977; Piaget 1966; Safar 1974).

The above research also demonstrates that various aspects of logico-mathematical knowledge develop together. For example, the groups of children who conserve number earlier also conserve other quantities and class-include earlier. Children thus do not construct number in isolation, apart from the rest of their logico-mathematical knowledge. Since logico-mathematical knowledge is constructed by children's putting things into relationships, it is not surprising that those who put objects into one kind of relationship also put them into many other kinds of relationships.

How *precisely* the child constructs number is still a mystery, just as the child's learning of language is still a mystery. However, there is enough theoretical and empirical evidence that shows the roots of number to be very general in nature. Since the notion of number can emerge only out of the child's putting all kinds of things into all kinds of relationships, the first principle of teaching is the importance of encouraging children to be alert and put all kinds of objects, events, and actions into all kinds of relationships (see Chapter 3).

The representation of number concepts

Once the child has built the logico-mathematical knowledge of *seven* or *eight,* he has the possibility of representing this idea either with symbols or with signs. In Piaget's theory, symbols are different from signs in that symbols bear a figurative resemblance to the objects being represented and are created by the child. An example of symbols is "o o o o o o o" or " IIIIIII ." Examples of signs are the spoken word *eight* and the written numeral *8.* Unlike symbols, signs are created by convention and do not bear any resemblance to the objects being represented. The reader may recognize signs as belonging to social knowledge.

Representation with signs is overemphasized in early childhood education and I prefer to put it in the background. Teachers too often teach children to count and to read and write numerals, believing that they are thereby teaching number concepts. It is good for children to learn to count and to read and write numerals, but a more important objective is for the child to construct the mental structure of number. If a child has constructed this structure, he will be able to assimilate signs into it with the greatest of ease. If he has not constructed it, all the counting and reading and writing of numerals can only be by rote.

While I prefer to deemphasize the teaching of signs, I also feel that it is good to teach them if children are genuinely interested in learning them. In reading, there must be things to read in the environment if the child is to become interested in reading. When he becomes interested in reading at whatever age, it is best to satisfy his curiosity and pride in acquiring new knowledge. Counting is likewise a joy for most preschool and kindergarten children, and if children want to learn to count, there is no reason to refuse this knowledge. The teacher must, however, know the difference between counting by rote and counting with numerical meaning. The numerical meaning can come only from the logico-mathematical structure constructed by the child in his head. All the spoken and written signs in the world are only surface knowledge. While there must be spoken and written numbers in the environment for the child to become interested in them, understanding them can come only from the mental structure that he constructs from within.[16]

In conclusion, the objective for "teaching" number is the child's construction of the mental structure of number. Since this structure cannot be taught directly, the teacher must focus on encouraging the child to think actively and autonomously in all kinds of situations. A child who thinks actively in his own way about all kinds of objects and events, including quantities, will inevitably construct number. The task of the teacher is to encourage the child's thinking in his own way, which is very difficult because most of us were trained to get children to produce "right" answers. Some principles of teaching to achieve this goal will be discussed in Chapter 3.

---

[16]F. Siegrist, A. Sinclair, and H. Sinclair are conducting research in Geneva on the ideas young children have about numerals at ages four to six, before first grade. Numerals are everywhere in the environment—on houses, buses, cans and boxes, price tags, football players' uniforms, license plates, etc.

3

Principles of teaching

In the following discussion, I will speak of "teaching number" even though number is not directly teachable. The reason for the use of this term is that the environment can do many things in indirect ways, as stated above, to foster the development of logico-mathematical knowledge, and I will, therefore, use the term "teach" as shorthand to refer to *indirect* teaching. Indirect teaching can vary from encouraging the child to put all kinds of things into all kinds of relationships, to asking him to get just enough plates for everybody at his table.

Six principles of teaching are presented under three headings that represent different perspectives. Under the first heading, I give the principle already discussed above: encouraging the child to put all kinds of things into all kinds of relationships. The second perspective focuses more specifically on the quantification of objects. The third concerns the child's social interaction with peers and teachers.

1. The creation of all kinds of relationships
   Encourage the child to be alert and to put all kinds of objects, events, and actions into all kinds of relationships.

2. The quantification of objects
   a. Encourage the child to think about number and quantities of objects when these are meaningful to him.
   b. Encourage the child to quantify objects logically and to compare sets (rather than encouraging him to count).
   c. Encourage the child to make sets with movable objects.

3. Social interaction with peers and teachers
   a. Encourage the child to exchange ideas with his peers.
   b. Figure out how the child is thinking, and intervene according to what seems to be going on in his head.

1. Encourage the child to be alert and to put all kinds of objects, events, and actions into all kinds of relationships

When an educator becomes aware of Piaget's theory of number, the first tendency is to think of its pedagogical implications within the realm of number. I, too, began by thinking in this way, and *Piaget, Children, and Number* (Kamii and DeVries 1976) reflects this limited view. The importance of creating and coordinating all kinds of relationships became clear as I personally reconstructed Piaget's theory as a whole. His research on space (Piaget and Inhelder 1948; Piaget, Inhelder, and Szeminska 1948), time (Piaget 1946), causality (Piaget and Garcia 1971), physical quantities (Piaget and Inhelder 1941), number (Piaget and Szeminska 1941), logic (Inhelder and Piaget 1955; 1959), mental imagery (Piaget and Inhelder 1966), moral development (Piaget 1932), animism and artificialism (Piaget 1926), etc., etc. at first seemed to concern only each distinct realm independently of the others. Many years later, I came to understand that, in reality, concrete operations develop in many areas simultaneously, and that Piaget and his collaborators published one book after another on different topics only because they could not study all aspects at the same time. When I finally understood the indissociability of this development, it became clear that the most important objective for educators is to encourage the child to put all kinds of objects, events, and actions into all kinds of relationships.

The following example illustrates the simultaneous construction of many kinds of relationships in real life. When I visited a kindergarten room at lunch time one day, a six-year-old boy suddenly turned around in his chair and accidentally pushed a plateful of salad off the table with his elbow. I asked him if he wanted me to help clean it up, and he responded with a resolute "No." He got up looking for something and came back with a large broom. When he was about to begin sweeping with it, I told him that I did not think that was a good idea because the salad dressing would spoil the broom and make it unusable. I told him that paper towels or napkins might work better and again offered to help him. He said, "No, I want to do it by myself." He got a generous supply of paper napkins and neatly cleaned up the mess by making one ball after another with each napkin. He lined them up on the table as he made them, went to get the garbage can, and carefully dropped each one into it as he counted them (five balls).

Many kinds of relationships were involved in this situation, and much learning took place. Interpersonal relationships and moral judgment were obviously involved, and I was thoroughly impressed with the autonomy of this six-year-old. (The teacher who had fostered this autonomy deserves recognition.) First of all, this experience made the child put his body into spatial relationship with the objects on the table that can be knocked off. The child obviously had no idea that the salad dressing would ruin the broom (or necessitate washing it). He may have learned that a certain type of object (absorbent paper) is better for cleaning up a certain type of mess (physical and social knowledge). Quantification was also involved when he counted five paper balls and had to put the rest of the napkins back.

Children who think actively in everyday living thus think about many things simultaneously. A passive, heteronomous child might have continued to sit there eating what was left. Note that the child did all kinds of thinking by himself. Relationships are created by the child from within, and not taught by someone else from the outside. The teacher has a crucial role, however, in creating the social and material environment that encourages autonomy and thinking. This child obviously wanted to clean the mess by himself and thought about many things because he had a goal for himself. Teachers who can promote the development of such autonomy in young children are rare.

The reader may remember the anecdote I told earlier about my niece and Santa Claus. This busy mind put not only wrapping paper and handwriting into relationship with Santa Claus but also the number of presents she and her brother had received. She counted her presents several times every day and said, for example, that she had only six yesterday but eight today because so-and-so gave her two today. She also counted her younger brother's presents and announced the number to be the same as hers each time.

Note that the child was not told to put types of wrapping paper or quantities into relationships. But she made unexpected inferences when she noticed that two presents wrapped in the same paper came from one person, and six others having different wraps came from six different people. I would like to point out the importance of the general atmosphere of the environment. If adults create an atmosphere that indirectly encourages thinking, children come up with a host of relationships that surprise us.[17]

Situations of conflict can encourage the child to put things into

---

[17]Most of us can think of examples such as the following: When a child watched a person pray for the first time before dinner, he asked, "Why does Grandpa read his plate?"

relationships. A child at a day care center protested one afternoon that the teacher was breaking her promise to let her go outside after nap. It had unexpectedly begun to rain while the children were asleep, and they knew that they never went outside when it rained. The child complained because she put only two events into relationship, i.e., the original promise and the later prohibition (which were not equal). A promise made under certain circumstances can sometimes not be kept when conditions change. "After nap" and "when it rains" are two sets of circumstances overlapping in part that have to be coordinated with the promise made earlier. Such intersections can be found all the time in daily living. Moral judgment and logical thinking develop together when children are encouraged to discuss the desirability or justifiability of a decision.

Negotiations in situations of conflict are particularly good for putting things into relationship and developing mobility and coherence of thought. To negotiate mutually acceptable solutions, the child has to decenter and imagine how the other person is thinking. A child raised in an authoritarian family has much fewer occasions to develop his ability to reason logically. Such a child is forced to obey rather than being encouraged to invent arguments that make sense and are convincing.

When two children fight over a toy, for example, the teacher can intervene in ways that promote or hinder children's thinking. If she says, "I'll have to take it away from both of you because you are fighting," the problem is quickly solved but children's thinking is not encouraged. Alternatively, the teacher can say, "I have an idea. What if I put it up on the shelf until you decide what to do? When you decide, you tell me, and I'll take it down for you." Children who are thus encouraged to make decisions are encouraged to think. They may decide that neither should get the toy, in which case the solution would be the same as the one imposed by the teacher. However, it makes an enormous difference from the standpoint of children's development of autonomy if they are encouraged to make decisions for themselves. This autonomy is indissociably social, moral, and intellectual. An alternative solution might be for one child to have the toy first and for the other to have it afterward. Traditional "math concepts" such as first-second, before-after, and one-to-one correspondence are part of the relationships children create in everyday living when they are encouraged to think.

Let us go on to three principles of teaching that involve more specifically the quantification of objects.

2(a). Encourage the child to think about number and quantities of objects when these are meaningful to him

If autonomy is the aim of education and the child must be mentally active to construct number, he must be encouraged to act out of his own choice and conviction rather than docility or obedience. I, therefore, do not advocate setting a time of day aside for the quantification of objects. Rather than doing math because the teacher says it is math time, children should be encouraged to think about quantities when they feel a need and interest. Almost all children between four and six years of age seem to be interested in counting objects and comparing quantities. As shown in the first principle of teaching, they spontaneously count the paper balls they make, the presents they receive, the candles on a cake, etc. They also argue about who has more blocks. When we watch them in bowling and marble games as well as dice and card games that require counting and/or addition, we become convinced that numerical thinking can develop naturally without any artificial lessons.

2(b). Encourage the child to quantify objects logically and to compare sets (rather than encouraging him to count)

When a teacher asks a child to bring cups for everybody at the table, she can say either "Would you bring six cups" or "Would you bring *just* enough cups for everybody." The latter is an example of language that involves logical quantification. This is a better request because it lets the child choose the best way for him to accomplish the task. When we ask the child to bring six cups, we tell him exactly what to do without thinking. Let us look at an example cited by Gréco (1962, p. 46), a long-time associate of Piaget, that illustrates the importance of letting the child choose the best way for him.

A mother asked her 5-year-old to put a napkin on everybody's plate for the main meal every day. There were regularly four people at the table. Jean-Pierre knew how to count to 30 or more. However, he went to the cupboard to take out the first napkin which he put on a plate, returned to the cupboard to take out the second napkin which he put on the second plate, and so on, making a total of four trips. At 5 years 3 months and 16 days, he spontaneously thought about counting the plates, counted four napkins to take out of the cupboard, and distributed them at the table. He proceeded in this way for six days.

On the seventh day, there was a guest and one more plate than usual. Jean-Pierre took his four napkins as usual, distributed them, and noticed that one plate remained empty. Instead of getting an additional napkin, he collected the four already on the plates, and put them back in the cupboard. He then began all over again and made five trips to accomplish the task.

The next day, the guest was not there, but Jean-Pierre continued to make four trips, and continued the same thing for five more days, until he rediscovered counting. After using this method for ten days, Jean-Pierre was told that there was a guest again. He distributed his four napkins as usual, but this time simply went to get the missing napkin when he saw the empty plate. The next day, when there were only four people again, he counted the number of plates before fetching the same number of napkins. The arrival of a new guest never bothered him after that.

We see in the above example the difference between mechanical counting and *counting chosen by the child* to solve a real problem. Knowing how to count is one thing. Knowing what to do when faced with an additional plate is quite another thing. If Jean-Pierre had been told the count the plates and napkins, he would have learned to depend on others to know what to do. Because he did not have precise instruction, he had a chance to develop his intellectual autonomy and self-reliance.

Saying that the child has to construct his own knowledge does not imply that the teacher must sit back and leave the child entirely alone. Like Jean-Pierre's mother, the teacher can create an environment in which the child has an important role and the possibility of deciding for himself how to carry out the responsibility that he freely accepted. Below are examples of other expressions like *just enough* that require the comparison of sets:

—Did you get *as many* cards as I did (or *the same number* or *the same amount*)?
—Do we have *too many* cups?
—Do we play *(Musical Chairs)* with *more* chairs, *fewer*, or *the same number*?
—Bobby has *less* than you do. Would you like to do something about that?
—Who has *the most*?

Again, the teacher must be careful not to insist that children give correct answers at all costs. These questions must be raised casually to encourage children to think numerically if this is of interest to them. In a card game, for example, if the teacher asks whether or not everybody got the same number of cards, the pursuit of this question must be stopped if the children react with indifference. The imposition of adult ideas in such situations cannot be justified any more than the imposition of lessons.

Counting is not unimportant. It is, in fact, essential for children to learn to count if they are to go on to addition. Research shows, however, that ability to say the number words is one thing and using this skill is quite another thing. I will summarize some of the research findings to show why it is important for teachers to focus on logico-mathematical thinking rather than on counting. The first set of studies by Gréco (1962) and Meljac (1979) shows that children before the age of seven who know how to count do not necessarily choose to use this skill when asked to put out the same number as the researcher. The second study, also by Meljac, shows that if children do not use counting as a tool, they have good reasons for not using it. Counting does not become a perfectly dependable tool for young children until the age of six.

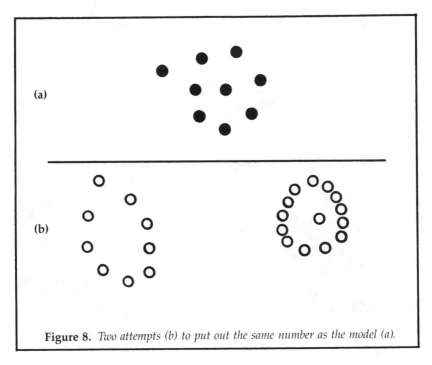

Figure 8. *Two attempts (b) to put out the same number as the model (a).*

Gréco showed nine chips arranged as shown in Figure 8(a) and asked children to put out the same number. The children ranged in age from four to eight. All of them knew how to count, some only to 10 and others to more than 30. As can be seen in Table 2, he found four levels,

Age group	Number of children	Level			
		0	I	II	III
4;6–5	10	6	4		
5–5;6	10		8	2	
5;6–6	10	1	2	4	3 (30%)
6–6;6	15		2	9	4 (26%)
6;6–7	10		4	4	2 (20%)
7–7;6	10		1		9 (90%)
7;6–8	10			4	6 (60%)
8–8;6	10				10 (100%)
Total	85	7	21	23	34

Table 2. *Relationship between age and level on quantification task reported by Gréco (1962).*

Age group	Number of children	Level			
		0	I	II	III
4–4;6	20	3	13	4	
5–5;6	22	4	8	4	6 (27%)
6–6;6	32	2	5	10	15 (47%)
7 years	11			5	6 (55%)
Total	85	9	26	23	27

Table 3. *Relationship between age and level on quantification task reported by Meljac (1979).*

the last one of which involved counting and was attained around the age of seven. The four levels are:

Level 0: Inability even to understand the adult's request

Level I: Rough, visual estimation or copy of the spatial configuration
At about five-and-one-half years of age, two behaviors are typical: the rough, perceptual estimation of a handful having about the same amount, and a rough figural copy such as the ones shown in Figure 8(b).

Level II: Methodical one-to-one correspondence
At level I, the children rarely look at the model while putting out the chips. At level II, they look alternately at the model and copy, even to the extent of using fingers to point at the corresponding elements each time.

Level III: Counting
The child counts the number in the model and then counts out the same number.

This study confirms the point made about Jean-Pierre. Children may know how to recite numbers in correct sequence, but they do not necessarily choose to use it as a dependable tool. When a child has constructed the mental structure of number and has assimilated the words into this structure, counting becomes a reliable tool. Before seven years of age, however, one-to-one correspondence, the copying of the spatial configuration, or even rough estimates are surer ways for the child to use. In a replication of this study, Meljac found essentially the same results as can be seen in Table 3.

Meljac's second study shows that if young children do not choose counting, they have good reasons for not choosing it. She specifically asked children to count nine circles pasted on a card, and found that they counted them perfectly only at age six as seen in Table 4. Before this age, the words sometimes went faster than the finger that pointed to the objects arranged in a line, and sometimes more slowly. If the objects were not arranged in a line, the children skipped one or more objects and/or counted the same one(s) more than once (see Figure 4(a)).

The significance of the preceding research for educators is that there is a progression from the first to the third abilities listed below, and that this development depends on the construction of the underlying mental structure of number and its coordination with the string of words

Age	Proportion
4 years	0%
4;6	40 (?)*
5 years	54
5;6	60
6 years (kindergarten)	100
6 years (elementary school)	90
6;6	100
7 years	100

*These children did not always count correctly.

Table 4. *The proportion of children at various ages who counted nine objects correctly.*

learned from the outside.

1. The ability to say the words in correct sequence
2. The ability to count objects (i.e., to make a one-to-one correspondence between the words and objects)
3. The choice of counting as the most desirable tool

Teachers trained without knowledge of Piaget's theory can often be seen teaching children to touch each object as they say a word. This is the teaching only of surface behavior. The child has to assimilate number words into the mental structure shown in Figure 5(b). If this structure is not yet constructed, the child does not have what he needs to assimilate number words. Teaching surface behavior in such a situation can serve only to make the child more docile. Letting him decide when to use counting results in the avoidance of such forcing and a more solid foundation for later learning.

2(c). Encourage the child to make sets with movable objects

When we ask children to focus on only one set of objects, we are limited to questions such as "How many are there?" and "Can you give me eight?" As explained in the preceding principle, asking children to count is not a good way to help them quantify objects. A better approach is to ask them to compare two sets.

There are two ways of asking children to compare two sets: by asking them to *make a judgment* about the equality or inequality of sets that are already made, and by asking them to *make a set*. The second approach is far better for two reasons. First, when we ask a child to make a judgment about two sets that are already made, the child's reason for comparing them is only that the adult wants an answer. Second, comparing ready-made sets is a passive activity in which the child is limited to only three possible responses: The two sets are the same, one has more, or the other has more.

When the child has to *make* a set, in contrast, as when he is asked to bring just enough cups for everyone at the table, he starts with zero, takes one, one more, one more, etc., until *he decides when to stop.* This kind of decision has more educational value because the child has to start at zero and decide exactly when to stop the action of adding one more.

The value of encouraging children to make sets implies that some commonly used materials are inappropriate for teaching elementary number. Workbook pictures such as the one in Figure 9 and Cuisenaire rods (Kunz 1965) are examples of such unfortunate materials.

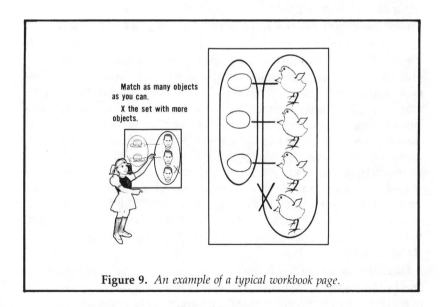

Figure 9. *An example of a typical workbook page.*

These workbook exercises are undesirable because they preclude any possibility for the child to move the objects to make a set. Besides, such an exercise easily elicits the kind of thinking that yields the right answer for the wrong reason. For example, when asked how they got the right answer in the exercise in Figure 9, many children explain, "You draw lines like this, and you put an X on the thing that doesn't have a line." Such children may or may not have the slightest idea about which set has *more*. If they do, this is usually because they already know how to tell which set has more. If they do not know how to tell this difference, the exercise is useless because children do not learn to make quantitative judgments by drawing lines on paper. The card game of *War* (see p. 64) permits children to compare ready-made sets much more intelligently than through this worksheet.

Children do not learn number concepts with pictures. They do not learn number concepts merely by manipulating objects either. They build these concepts by reflective abstraction as they act (mentally) on objects. When Jean-Pierre was getting napkins out, for example, the important thing was not the manipulation of objects but the thinking that was taking place as he tried to decide what to do with the napkins in relation to the plates and people involved. Once children construct the logic of one-to-one correspondence (by reflective abstraction), pictures like those in Figure 9 are completely superfluous.

It is important for the teacher to know that there is a world of difference between putting a napkin on each plate and thinking about the number of napkins in relation to the number of plates. The former is only an observable, spatial placement of one napkin on each plate. This relationship between *single objects* is not the same thing as the relationship between *groups of objects*. Putting a napkin on each plate lets the child know only that there is a napkin on each plate. When Jean-Pierre decided to count the plates, by contrast, he was thinking about the group of plates and the group of napkins. The child who thinks of counting the plates to know how many napkins to get is using counting very differently from one who counts them after being told to do so. The latter is mechanically following a procedure. The former thought of using counting as a middle term by reasoning that if $P = n$ and $N = n$, then $P = N$ (where P stands for plates, N stands for napkins, and n stands for a number).

Further criticism of worksheets can be found in the next principle, and I would now like to turn to Cuisenaire rods. Cuisenaire's approach to teaching number with rods reflects failure to differentiate discrete and continuous quantities. For Cuisenaire, the 1-cm rod stands for *1*, the 5-cm rod stands for *5*, and the 10-cm rod stands for *10*. For young children, however, each of these rods can only be *1*, since it is a single, discrete object. Number involves the quantification of discrete objects, and therefore cannot be taught through length, which is a continuous quantity.[18] Giving such ready-made 2, 3, 4, etc., to young children is worse than giving them ready-made sets such as those in Figure 9. This picture at least shows discrete objects.

Montessori (1912), Stern (Stern and Stern 1971), and many others, too, made seriated rods proportioned according to the same principle as Cuisenaire rods. This principle is to make the second rod twice as long as the first one, the third one three times as long as the first, etc. Advocates of teaching number with such rods believe that by ordering the rods and counting the segments, children learn the number series, including the idea that 1 is included in 2, 2 is included in 3, etc. Piaget and his collaborators' research (Inhelder and Piaget 1959, Chapter 9) shows that, in reality, when the child learns to arrange the rods from the longest to the shortest, or vice versa, all he learns is the empirical trick of using the stairstep shape to judge whether or not his arrangement is correct. This shape is an observable spatial configuration that the child can use as a source of external feedback. In logico-mathematical knowledge, however, feedback can come only from the internal consistency of a logical system constructed by the child. This system is not observable. It is constructed by the child's coordination of differences that are not observable either.[19] Ability to arrange objects by trial and error based on feedback from the configuration is thus very different from the ability to think logically by coordinating the differences among objects.

Let us go on to the third group of principles concerning the child's social interaction with peers and adults.

---

[18]A continuous quantity such as a length can be quantified only by introducing an arbitrary unit that is not given in the object. The logical structure of order and hierarchical inclusion is the same in number and in the measurement of length. In number, however, the unit is given by the object. For the teaching of beginning elementary number, therefore, continuous quantities are inappropriate. (Once the child has constructed number, however, Cuisenaire rods may be useful to visualize commutativity, set partitioning, etc. Once he has the idea of 1, 5, or 10, he can impose it on a rod.)

[19]An example of "the coordination of difference" is the following (where "A, B, C, D, . . . , and J" stand for ten sticks): If A>B, B>C, C>D, . . . , and I>J, then A>J. When a child has constructed such a logical system in which all the differences among the sticks can be coordinated simultaneously, he arranges the sticks *systematically* by looking for the longest one (A), the next longest one (B), etc. When he does not have such a system, however, he proceeds *by trial and error* and bases his judgment on the stairstep shape of the arrangement. See Gillièron (1977) for more research.

3(a). *Encourage the child to exchange ideas with his peers*

As stated above, arithmetic does not have to be transmitted from one generation to the next like social (conventional) knowledge, since logico-mathematical knowledge is constructed by the child's coordination of relationships, and nothing is arbitrary in this coordination. In logico-mathematical knowledge, if children argue long enough, they will sooner or later find the truth without any teaching or correction by the teacher. For example, in a card game, if a child says that $2 + 4 = 5$, he will eventually find the truth if he argues long enough with other players who do not agree with him.

A fundamental principle of teaching in the logico-mathematical realm, therefore, is to avoid both the reinforcement of the correct answer and the correction of wrong answers, and to encourage, instead, the exchange of ideas among children. If a child says that $2 + 4 = 5$, the best reaction is to say, "Does everybody agree?" If no one has any other idea, it may be best to drop the question. Silence in such a situation usually means that the question was too hard for everybody. When a child brings "just enough straws . . . ," similarly, the best thing for the teacher to do is to refrain from giving direct feedback as to the correctness of the response. After the child distributes the straws, he or someone else will observe the outcome. When a child is confronted with another child's idea that conflicts with his, he is usually motivated to think about the problem again, and either revise his idea or find an argument to defend it.

When we teach number and arithmetic as if adults were the only valid source of feedback, we unintentionally teach that truth can come only from us. The child then learns to read in the teacher's face signs of approval and disapproval. Such instruction reinforces the child's heteronomy and results in his learning to conform to adult authority. It is not in this way that children will develop knowledge of number, autonomy, or confidence in their mathematical ability. Piaget (1948) vigorously opposed this kind of teaching and insisted that the emotional block many students develop about math is completely avoidable.

I stated earlier that the source of feedback in logico-mathematical knowledge is the internal coherence of the logical system constructed by the child. Although the ultimate source of feedback is inside the child, disagreement with other children can stimulate him to reexamine his own ideas. When he argues that $2 + 4 = 5$, for example, the child has an opportunity to think about the correctness of his own thinking if he wants to convince somebody else. This is why social confrontation among peers is indispensable for the development of logico-mathematical knowledge.

The importance of social interaction was demonstrated by Perret-Clermont (1980). In experiments with groups of three children each time, she proved that the clashes of opinions and efforts to resolve a disagreement during ten minutes can stimulate the preoperational-level child to make new relationships and reason at a higher level than children in the control group (who did not have such an opportunity). It is simply not true that children have to be instructed or corrected by someone who knows more than they do. In the logico-mathematical realm, the confrontation of two wrong ideas can give rise to an idea that is more logical than either of the two. For example, if one child thinks that $2 + 4 = 5$ and another that $2 + 4 = 4$, both may correct their reasoning while trying to convince the other that they are right.

Group games, that are discussed here and elsewhere (Kamii and DeVries 1980), are ideal situations for the exchange of opinions among children. In group games children are motivated to check everybody else's counting and addition, to be able to confront those who cheat or make a mistake. Correcting and being corrected by peers in group games are far better than what can be learned through worksheets. When children mark worksheets, they do only their own work and do not check each other's thinking. When they finish the sheet, furthermore, they turn it over to the teacher to judge the correctness of each answer. Such dependence on adult authority is bad for the child's development of autonomy as well as logic. In group games children are mentally much more active and critical, and they learn to depend on themselves to know whether or not their reasoning is correct.

3(b). Figure out how the child is thinking, and intervene according to what seems to be going on in his head

If children make errors, this is usually because they are using their intelligence in their own way. Since every error is a reflection of the child's thinking, the teacher's task is not to correct the answer, but to figure out how the child made the error. Based on this understanding, the teacher can sometimes correct the process of reasoning which is far better than correcting the answer. For example, if the child brings one fewer than just enough cups, the reason may be that he did not count himself. Preoperational-level children often have difficulty considering themselves as both the counter and the counted. When they count the others, therefore, they frequently do not count themselves. When they distribute cups and find they are one short, a casual question such as "Did you count yourself when you counted the children?" may be helpful.

Just as there are many ways of getting the wrong answer, there are many ways of getting the right answer. One illustration of this is a study by Piaget and Szeminska (1941, Chapter 8) of how children divide 18 counters between two people. They found three different ways (levels) of getting the right answer, only the last one of which is based on logical reasoning. The three approaches follow.

1. An intuitive (global) approach

   The child divides the counters in a rough, global way and may by accident give nine to each person. This is an example of getting the right answer by chance. After thus dividing the counters, the child may end up saying that there are more in one bunch, especially if the spatial configuration is changed as shown in Figure 10(a).

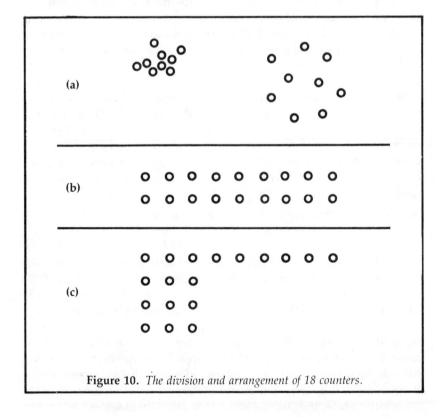

Figure 10. *The division and arrangement of 18 counters.*

2. A spatial approach

    The child spatially puts the counters in one-to-one correspondence as shown in Figure 10(b). After thus dividing the counters, he may end up saying that there are more in one set if one of the arrangements is changed as shown in Figure 10(c).

3. A logical approach

    The child gives one (or more) to each person alternately until all 18 of the counters are exhausted. The spatial arrangement becomes irrelevant when the child's logic is well developed. When the procedure used is thus logical, the child can do the task with his eyes closed. After dealing 40 cards to two players, these children are so sure of their procedure that they do not need to count the cards to know with certitude that the two received the same number.

By observing the child's behavior, the alert teacher can infer whether the child is approaching a problem in an intuitive, spatial, or logical way. On the basis of this kind of continuous observation, the teacher can intervene to influence the child's process of thinking instead of responding to the answer.

In a room of beginning first graders, a teacher noticed that a child was dividing the cards by the intuitive method to play *War.* She gave about half of the deck to herself and the rest to her opponent, in a stack. She then compared the height of the two stacks to make sure she had divided the cards satisfactorily. The teacher here did not correct the child because such correction would have stifled the pupil's initiative. Besides, she knew that the child would soon invent a better way anyway, and that making her deal cards correctly would only produce surface compliance. Furthermore, young children usually do not care about the exact number of cards they have at the beginning of a game. All they care about is to begin playing.

In children's distribution of cards, I have never seen the second level, i.e., spatial one-to-one correspondence. Children usually deal cards by giving one to each player, but this is often a mere imitation of behavior. When they can be distracted easily and/or skip a child or give two cards in succession to the same player, these behaviors reflect the absence of a feeling of logical necessity about following a strict procedure.

The teacher in Photograph 3 has the above three approaches in mind, in addition to a fourth—counting. The four-year-old in charge of the snack here has to put out enough cups and napkins for everybody at her table and give the same number of crackers to everybody. There is no shortage of supervisors, and the teacher refrains from intervening. She is wondering if and when one of the children might notice the unequal quantities of crackers. If no one notices anything wrong, there is no point in correcting the child in charge.

Photograph 3. *Getting the snack ready.*
The child in charge is expected to get out enough cups and napkins for everybody at her table, and to give the same amount of crackers to everybody.

In a room of five- and six-year-olds, I observed the following division of raisins and a teacher who reacted in accord with the way the children were thinking. She served a heap of raisins in a bowl for snack, with pieces of cheese. When everybody was ready to eat at the table, one child asked, "How many raisins do we take?" The teacher replied, "I think each table can decide how many you can take." The next question raised by a child was "Can we take six?" The teacher answered, "What do you think? Do you think that idea will work?" "I don't know, we'll have to see," was the response, and the children each took six. There were many raisins left afterward, and someone suggested taking three. The bowl went around once more, and there were still many left in it.

One child had been in the bathroom and joined the group at this time. "How many do I take?" she asked. The answer she got from a friend was "You take six first and then three." The teacher took advantage of this conversation to ask "How many is that altogether?" This question was greeted with silence. Wisely, she did not push her lesson, as the children were obviously not interested in it. Addition was too hard for these children. Someone then suggested, "Everybody can take ten now," and two children protested that there were not enough left for everybody to have ten. The teacher encouraged this exchange of ideas, and the group decided to try taking ten. After three children each took ten, the bowl was almost empty. The teacher remarked, "I guess that wasn't such a good idea," and the inventor of the idea pretended not to hear. Fortunately, the rest of the children did not seem to care about raisins any more. Children usually care more about food than other objects to divide, but at times even food is of no interest to them.

I now turn from general principles of teaching to specific classroom situations that lend themselves particularly well to the "teaching" of number.

4

Situations in school that the teacher can use to "teach" number

Before discussing specific situations that the teacher can use to stimulate children's numerical thinking, I would like to remind the reader once more that the child does not construct number outside the context of thinking in general throughout the day. The teacher must, therefore, encourage the child to put all kinds of things, ideas, and events into relationships all the time rather than focusing only on quantification. The following examples of quantification are given on the assumption that such a context exists.

The situations conducive to the quantification of objects are presented under two headings—daily living and group games. I hope the reader will see in each example an expression of Principle 2(a), Encourage the child to think about number and quantities of objects when these are meaningful to him.

Daily living

Quantification constitutes an inevitable part of daily living. For example, paper cups, and napkins have to be distributed, things have to be divided fairly among the children, and pieces of board games must not be lost. These responsibilities are often carried out by the teacher on the assumption that children are too young for these chores when they are four to six years of age. With a bit of organization, the teacher can give these tasks to children, at least in part, and create situations in which quantification can take place in a natural and meaningful way. The situations discussed below are the distribution of materials, the division of objects, the collection of objects, the recording of information, cleanup, and voting.

The distribution of materials

In Principles 2(b) and 2(c), I gave the example of asking children to bring "just enough cups for everybody at your table." When children cannot deal with the total number of pupils in the class, the teacher can divide the large group into small ones so that the number in each will be small enough for the children to handle. The request to bring "just enough for everybody at your table" is particularly meaningful when the number of objects available (e.g., scissors) is exactly the same as the total number of children in the entire class.

As stated in the discussion of Principle 3(b), children who can use counting in other situations are sometimes unsuccessful in distributing objects because they forget to count themselves. The child who did the counting will clearly see that he did not bring enough. The teacher's task will then be to use this observation casually, in a positive way, as discussed in Principle 3(a) (Encourage the child to exchange ideas with his peers.).

The division of objects

Snack time presents the problem of dividing raisins, apple slices, or other foods in a fair way as seen in the examples given to illustrate Principle 3(b). When the child distributes a certain number of objects, he knows ahead of time how many he has to give to each person. When he divides them, however, he does not know the number he should give to each person. Rather than taking a subset from a large set, the child must break the large set up into many equal subsets when he divides a group of objects.

Again, this task is too hard if one child has to divide things among all the children in the class. The teacher can, however, give a certain number to each pair of children (or to each group of three, four, etc.) to divide in a fair way. If a child protests that someone else got more, the teacher can follow Principles 3(a) and 3(b) and encourage children to exchange ideas to resolve the conflict. When the children propose a solution, their idea may or may not be fair from the teacher's point of view. For example, one child may say, "I'll give you some," and offer somebody else's share that looks like a larger quantity because of its spatial arrangement. In such a situation, it is best not to impose our adult view if all the children are satisfied. The imposition of the right answer that is incomprehensible from the child's point of view teaches him only to go along silently with the adult in power.

The collection of things

The collection of such things as parental permission slips prior to a field trip provides a natural opportunity for teaching the additive composition of number. At group time, the teacher may present the question of whether or not to call the bus company to make the final arrangement. Questions such as the following can also be posed:

—Do we have all the slips we need?
—How many more do we need to have?
—How many children brought their slips back yesterday?
—How many brought theirs back today?
—Who was absent yesterday? How many were absent?

As usual, if the task can be made more manageable by dividing the class into small groups, this is certainly worth doing. Small groups also offer the advantage of letting more children have a chance to exercise leadership.

When the teacher distributes the slips for the children to take home, he might say, "I will write on the chalkboard how many slips I gave out so I will know tomorrow how many to collect." The names of the children who are absent can also be written on the board. This, by the way, is a good example of an incidental, natural way of exposing children to reading and writing.

The collection of milk money may be too difficult, but children can at least help count the number who paid in order to know how many cartons to distribute later.

Keeping records

Figure 11 is an example of the kind of attendance record some young children can handle. If the number involved is small enough, even young children can mark their presence, the number present, and the number absent. This kind of chart can stimulate children's interest in reading their friends' names.

The teacher may also want to refer to the attendance chart to figure out with the children how many more permission slips or library books need to be collected. As usual, he must include in each chart no more names than the number that children can handle.

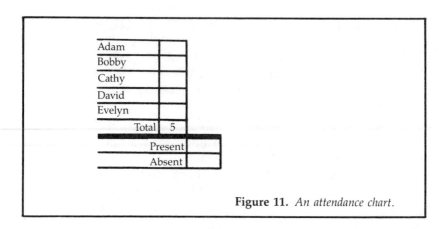

Figure 11. *An attendance chart.*

Cleanup

Various opportunities for numerical quantification can be found in the context of cleanup. For example, the teacher can label boxes as shown in Figure 12 so that children will know how many objects they should look for before putting a board game away.

If there is a general cleanup time, some teachers suggest that each person put three things away.

Some teachers have a chart showing who is responsible for cleaning up each of several areas of the room. At the beginning of cleanup, the entire class gets together, and each person in charge of an area decides how many helpers he wants and chooses helpers from those who have not been chosen. Each group can begin to clean up as soon as it has thus been organized.

Voting

On many occasions, the teacher can suggest that the group decide by majority vote (see Photograph 4). Voting is useful, for example, when the group cannot agree on what to name the gerbil or whether to plan biscuits or muffins for the next day's snack. While voting does teach the comparison of quantities, its more important function is to place the power of decision making in the hands of the children, thereby promoting their autonomy.

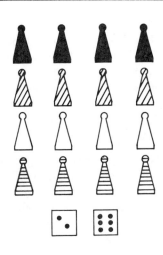

Figure 12. *A list of objects to look for before putting a game away.*

Photograph 4. *Voting to decide on the goldfish's name.*

   At the beginning of the year, four- and five-year-olds feel no need to vote for only one of the choices. Some vote twice, others three times! Given many opportunities to vote, however, they do not have to be reminded, by midyear, that they can vote for only one of the choices. They also propose a vote whenever a group decision has to be made.

Group games

As can be seen in Kamii and DeVries (1980), many group games provide an excellent context for thinking in general and for comparing quantities. Below are some examples of aiming games, hiding games, races and chasing games, guessing games, board games, and card games.

Aiming games

Marble games and bowling are particularly good for counting objects and comparing quantities (see Photographs 5 and 6). In these situations, children are motivated to know how many marbles they knocked out of the circle or how many pins fell over. However, the teacher must be careful not to insist that children compare their performances. At four years of age, children are interested only in what they are themselves doing. Only around five or six years of age do certain children

Photograph 5. *Marbles.*
These five-year-olds were interested only in rolling marbles out of the enclosure. When the teacher asked, "How many did you get out?" they ignored her completely. Wisely, the teacher dropped the question.

Photograph 6. *Bowling.*
Three-year-olds are usually not interested in knowing how many they knocked over. An occasional question like "How many do you still have to knock down?" may interest some children, but the teacher must be careful not to insist on getting an answer to this question.

begin to be interested in competition.[20] One note of caution: When a four- or five-year-old says, "I have seven and John has eight," he is not necessarily comparing the two sets. This statement is often a simple announcement of the result of counting.

It is better for children to be introduced to writing when this is useful and meaningful to them than when the teacher says for no apparent reason that it is now time to write answers on worksheets. Figures 13 and 14 are examples of score sheets kept in bowling games. Bowling necessitates scorekeeping if each child has more than one turn. Be-

[20]The reader is referred to Piaget (1932, Chapter 1) or to Kamii and DeVries (1980, Chapter 2) for more information about these developmental changes.

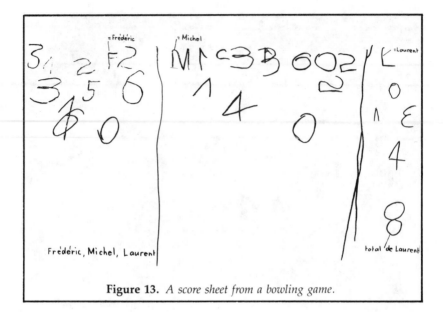

Figure 13. *A score sheet from a bowling game.*

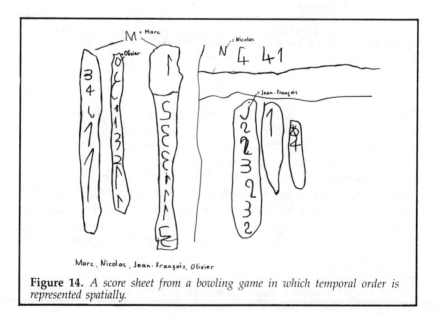

Figure 14. *A score sheet from a bowling game in which temporal order is represented spatially.*

cause each player uses the same set of pins, there is no trace left of the number knocked over if a record is not kept. Marble games are different. The players can keep the marbles they knocked out of the enclosure, and there is, therefore, no reason for them to keep a record.

Below are excerpts from the teacher's notes showing the context in which these score sheets were made (Capt, Glayre, and Hegyi 1976). As can be seen in these notes, development in arithmetic is indissociable from other aspects of development.

June 1975 (The children were about five years old.)

The children arranged the bowling pins[21] in a line, one against another, explaining that this way is "easier to knock them over."

At first they did not take turns. The one catching the ball was the one who threw it next. Later, they organized themselves into taking turns.

For each throw, they counted the number which fell down, without putting them into an additive relationship with the number they knocked down on the previous throw.

They do not feel any need to stand at a specific spot to throw the ball. Some stand far away from the target, some very close to it, and some at the side.

Later, they varied the spatial arrangement by lining up the bottles in straight lines and in circles and ovals.

September 1975

Another way of playing has appeared. The children arrange the pins spaced out in a line. Each time a pin falls over, they take it out of the game. When there is only one pin left, since aiming becomes difficult, they bring the pin closer and closer. The game has thus become more structured with the following rules:

> Arrange the pins on a line.
> Eliminate each that falls.
> Bring the last one closer.

January–February 1976 (The children were about six years of age and in kindergarten.)

The children now feel the need to draw a line beyond which they cannot go when they roll the ball, but there is no competition among them.

They now write numbers on paper, and some add up their total score. For example, Laurent's column shows that $0 + 1 + 3 + 4 = 8$ (as can be seen in Figure 13). The other children's "columns" are not as well structured. It is not clear from this sheet whether the three children had unequal numbers of turns, or whether some practiced writing numbers

---

[21]The bowling pins were plastic bottles used to sell mineral water in Switzerland. Mineral water is widely consumed there, and the teacher asked the children to bring the one-liter size their parents no longer needed. The children painted these bottles and filled them with sand.

in their "columns."
Another way of playing the game is to try to make all the pins fall, and to count the number of throws necessary to achieve this result.

May 1976

The children now organize themselves tightly before they begin the game. They decide how they will play and how they will keep score. Figure 14 is an example of the record kept by four players. The columns are much better structured than those in Figure 13, and space is used to represent the temporal sequence of the number knocked over. There is no zero on this sheet (the one *0* is Olivier's initial) because the following line of reasoning reigned.

Jean-François came to record a zero after he failed to knock any of the pins over.

Marc intervened, "No, you know, you don't need to make the zeros."

The teacher asked, "You don't write the zeros down?"

Marc explained, "No, you see, we don't need to because zero means 'nothing.' "

Vincent agreed, "That's right. Zero is 'nothing at all.' So we don't write it."

(*Des Activités de Connaissance Physique à l'Ecole Enfantine,* pp. 128–133)

Making the children write *0* in the above situation would have been unwise. Such an imposition would only have taught them to conform to arbitrary adult demands.

Hiding games

The teacher can introduce the game of hiding five oranges. The group is divided into two subgroups for this game, so that some children can hide the objects and the rest can try to find them.[22] When the latter have found three oranges, for example, they have to know how many more they have to look for. This game thus entails set partitioning, which involves addition and subtraction. In hide-and-seek, too, some children figure out how many more players remain to be found.

Another hiding game can be played with six tongue depressors. After showing the sticks to the children, the teacher hides all of them under the table with both hands, and then brings four out in one hand.

----

[22]Some teachers divide the class neatly into two equal groups, and say who should go out of the room and who should stay in to hide the oranges. A far better way for the development of children's autonomy and thinking is to ask, "Who wants to hide the oranges?" and "Who wants to find them?" Letting the children organize themselves and decide what to do next is much more educational than the teacher's directing the game. See Kamii and DeVries (1980) for an explantion of this point.

He then asks, "How many do you think are in my hand under the table?" When this game becomes too easy, the teacher can play a trick from time to time by hiding one or two sticks between his legs. This kind of trick gives children a chance to strengthen their power of reasoning.

Races and chasing games

Games such as *Musical Chairs*[23] and *Duck, Duck, Goose* involve the quantification and ordering of objects. In *Musical Chairs*, (Photograph 7) we can encourage children to figure out how many chairs they need. This game must not be played with the entire class. If children are

Photograph 7. *Musical Chairs.*
The most educational part of the game may be in progress here.

---

[23]*Musical Chairs* is usually played in the following way. Chairs numbering one less than the number of children are arranged in a line, back to back. When the music begins, all the children march around the chairs, and when it stops, everybody runs to sit on a chair. The one who does not get one is put out of the game. One chair is removed each time a child is put out. The player who sits on the last chair is the winner.

encouraged to begin their own games,[24] the number of players is generally rather small. The teacher can also make many small groups rather than one large group. For young children, the rules of the game must be modified so that no one will be eliminated. Interestingly enough, at four to five years of age, children usually prefer to play *Musical Chairs* with as many chairs as children. We must encourage them to exchange ideas to decide how they want to play this game— with the same number of chairs as children, or with one or more chairs fewer (but without eliminating those who did not get a chair). All of these variations are good for the quantification of objects.[25]

The most educational part of *Musical Chairs* may lie in its preparation. The teacher who arranges the chairs instead of letting children prepare the game deprives them of an ideal situation for deciding when they have gotten the desired number.

Duck, Duck, Goose is not a game that involves counting as such. However, it may be useful for the construction of number because the child has to put many elements (players) into the relationship of order. "It" goes around the circle touching the head of each child forming the circle. As he touches each child, he says "Duck." When he chooses a person to call "Goose," the "Goose" chases "It" around the circle, like in the game of dropping the handkerchief. The difficulty of putting the players in order can often be seen among four-year-olds, who do not feel the need to touch every child's head. When they say "Duck," they skip one or more without any sign of being bothered by this infraction. Older children, in contrast, are so careful not to skip anyone that they even feel obliged to go back and touch a player they overlooked.[26]

Group games present many opportunities to put things into all kinds of other relationships. In *Duck, Duck, Goose,* for example, children have a tendency to choose their friends or the popular children. This is an ideal situation to make a dichotomy between "those who have already had a turn" and "those who have not." The teacher must be diplomatic when he asks "It" to *try to* choose a player who has not

---

[24]The reader is strongly urged to refer to Kamii and DeVries (1980) for an elaboration of this principle of teaching and many others.

[25]Even after listening to a clear explanation of why there will be one child who will not get a chair, the three-year-old who does not get one is often surprised and perplexed when he finds that everybody has one except him. He often goes around looking for his chair! When this happens, the game is much too hard and must be avoided.

[26]In some groups, the children make up the rule that "It" has to go in the middle of the circle if he skips a child.

had a turn. If he is too categorical and declares that only those who have not had a turn will be chosen, the game deteriorates, since those who know they will not have a chance any more will become restless and uninterested in the activity.

A guessing game

"It" can take out one of the ten cards bearing numbers from 1 to 10. The other children try to guess which card was taken out. "It" responds to each guess by saying, "Yes," "No, it's more," or "No, it's less." For example, if the number taken out is 5, and the first guess is 10, the response will be "No, it's less." For those who want to keep a record of the numbers guessed, the chalkboard is a useful tool. Some advanced children write 1 2 3 4 5 6 7 8 9 10 and proceed by the process of elimination. Others write 1 2 3 . . . to keep a record of the number of guesses taken!

Board games

Games such as *Candy Land* (1955) and *Chutes and Ladders* (1956) can be found in stores, and parents buy them as gifts. In this type of game, three different ways are used to indicate a number: cards, a spinner, and one or more dice. Players have opportunities to advance toward the goal by taking the number of steps indicated by the card, spinner, or die. The teacher can make the game easier by using only small numbers up to three or four. He can also make it harder by using two or three dice.

In the above games, the cards, spinner, or die is used to indicate the number of steps to take rather than the number of objects to take. When the child takes steps with a marker, the point of departure disappears as soon as the first step is taken. Furthermore, quantification is not very clear when the segments are made up of units introduced into a continuous road. For children whose number concepts are still shaky, the teacher can make a different kind of game in light of Principle 2(c) (Encourage the child to make sets with movable objects). The game shown in Figure 15(a) uses a piece of cardboard divided into 12 squares, counters that can be placed on the squares, and a die. The object of the game is to be the first one to fill up the board, or to fill it up and then empty it by removing the number indicated on the die.

The above game allows the child simply to fill up the entire board, without the need to know how many squares there are. This feature is sometimes an advantage and sometimes a disadvantage. It is an ad-

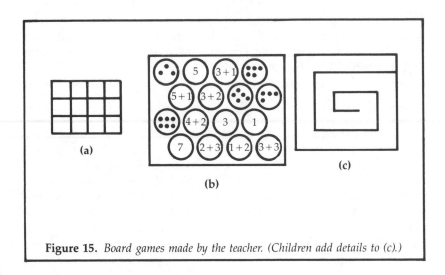

Figure 15. *Board games made by the teacher. (Children add details to (c).)*

Photograph 8. *All gone.*

Vegetable trays, pieces of Styrofoam packing material, and a die are used in this game. Starting with 20 pieces in each tray, players take turns throwing the die and taking that many pieces out. The person who empties his tray first is the winner.

vantage when children cannot yet quantify 12 objects. Because they can merely try to fill up the board, the children can play this game even if 12 is too big a number for them. When children have become able to quantify 12 objects, however, being able merely to fill up a card does not allow them to take maximum advantage of the situation. A possible modification to avoid this problem is to begin by putting 12 (or more) objects on a sheet of paper (or a tray) and remove each time the number indicated on the die. The player who gets rid of all his objects first is the winner. (See Photograph 8.)

Hi-Ho! Cherry-O (1972), that can be seen in Photograph 9, is an appealing game that uses exactly the same principle of removing the number of objects indicated by chance. It is, however, a more limited game because the number of cherries at the beginning of the game can only be ten. For most four-year-olds, this number is not too easy.

The game shown in Figure 15(b) is made with a Styrofoam board found in stores to display fruit. Children play the game by throwing one or more dice and trying to be the first one to fill up all the holes.

Until children have played various board games, the teacher may want to give the rules. Later, however, he can present a board such as the one shown in Figure 15(c) and ask children to invent a game. Those who want to start with a blank sheet of paper should, of course, be encouraged to invent their game without any help or constraint.

Card games

There are so many card games that are excellent for the development of logical and numerical thinking that I have to be selective and give only three examples: *Concentration, War,* and *Fives.* Other card games can be found in Kamii and DeVries (1980). *Card Dominoes,* which is excellent in kindergarten, is discussed in Kamii (1981). *Concentration* is the easiest of the three, and possible even for some three-year-olds. *War* is harder, and *Fives* is even harder than *War* because it involves addition. (Addition goes beyond the objectives for preschool and kindergarten discussed earlier. However, if a few advanced children are genuinely interested in it, they should certainly be encouraged to pursue this interest.)

In *Concentration* (Photograph 10), the cards are arranged in rows and columns, face down. The players try to find pairs that are the same by turning two cards over, trying to recall where they have seen specific pictures. If a player finds two identical cards, he can keep them and keep playing. If not, he has to turn the cards over as they were before, and it is the next person's turn. The player who collects the greatest

Photograph 9. *Hi-Ho! Cherry-O.*

The players begin by standing the trees up and hanging ten plastic cherries on their trees. (The teacher found that some children have difficulty making the cherries stay on the tree, and that it is easier if the trees are flat on the board as shown in this picture. Children can also see the cherries better this way.) In turn, each player spins the spinner to know how many cherries to take off his tree and put into his bucket. The person who gets all ten of his cherries off his tree first is the winner.

There is no problem of interpretation when the spinner points to 1, 2, 3, or 4 cherries. However, when it points to the segment showing 13 cherries spilling out of the basket, these three-year-olds interpret the picture simply as "a lot." "A lot" to some means four, while to others it means to take all 10! The rules of the game state that this picture means to put all the cherries in one's bucket back *on* the tree. To these children, however, the picture means to take a lot of cherries *off* their tree. Pictures do not have conventional meanings as words do, according to Piaget. It is, therefore, inappropriate to impose arbitrary meanings and rules, such as this one, that are foreign to the way children think. Whatever an individual sees in a picture is what the picture means *to him*. If a group of children disagrees on the meaning of a picture, each group must be allowed to come to an agreement of its own.

To many four-year-olds, likewise, the spinner pointing to the picture of a dog in this game means 4 "because dogs have four legs." Similarly, the picture of a bird means 2 "because birds have two legs." According to the printed rules, however, the bird and the dog both mean "Player takes two cherries from his pail and puts them back onto his tree." The imposition of such arbitrary rules is harmful for the child's development of autonomy.

number of pairs is the winner. (Young children count the number of cards rather than the number of pairs. Some compare the height of the piles. Others are not interested at all in comparing the number of cards won.)

Photograph 10. *Concentration.*

Two children are playing together, and one child is playing alone. As Piaget (1932) said, four-year-olds play either alone without bothering to find a partner or with a partner without trying to win. These children are not at all interested in *comparing* the number of cards they have at the end of the game, but *each child* tries hard to get as many as possible.

The simplest way of playing *War* (Photograph 11) is between two players who use cards that go only up to 10. The cards are dealt to the players, who keep them in a pile, face down. Each person then turns up the top card of his stack and the two compare the numbers. The one who has the greater of the two numbers takes both cards. The game continues in this way until the two piles are used up.[27] The person who collects more cards than the other is the winner.

As in *Concentration*, some children compare the height of the piles to determine who won. Others are not at all interested in comparing the number of cards won.

When the two cards turned up happen to have the same number, each player puts the next card on top of the first one, face down, and compares the third card turned up. The one who has the greater

Photograph 11. *War.*
The comparison of 6 and 7 requires more time (and counting at times) than the comparison of 2 and 8.

---

[27]Some children continue to play until one of them collects all the cards.

Photograph 12. *Piggy Bank*.
   Fives is a modification of this game (Ed-U-Cards 1965). This child modified the rule and eliminated dealing the cards. The players simply took turns picking up the top card of the stack. The child turned up a 1, tried 2 + 1, and concluded that he could not take any cards! If the next player turns up a 3, he can pick up four cards (2 + 3 and 4 + 1).

number then takes all six cards. (This rule can be modified to simplify the game. Instead of putting a second card face down before turning over a third card, the players can simply compare the second card.)
   Fives involves the set partitioning of 5. (See Photograph 12 which illustrates a similar game.) Eight cards each of numbers 1 through 4 are used (8 × 4 = 32 cards). (These can be homemade or taken from two decks of playing cards.) All the cards are dealt to two, three, or four players. Each player keeps his pile face down. When his turn comes, he turns his top card over and tries to make a total of 5 with another card. For example, if the first player discards a 2 and the second turns up a 3, the latter can take the 2 with his 3 and keep them (in a separate pile). If the second player turns up a 1, however, he, too, has to discard his card because 2 + 1 ≠ 5.[28] The player who collects the greatest number of

---

[28]The first player can never make a total of 5, as there are no cards on the table. Young children do not notice this disadvantage and want to be the first player!

cards is the winner.[29]

Concentration is the only one of the three games that can be played either with picture cards or with regular playing cards having numerals. For *Concentration*, however, picture cards are preferable for two reasons. First, the content is more interesting when pictures, rather than numbers, are matched. Second, pictures are usually more dissimilar than numbers, and it is easier to use a classificatory scheme to remember where a certain picture was last seen than to remember where a particular number was last seen. For example, the location of a boat or flower is easier to remember than the location of a 7 or a 4, 5, or 6.

The reader may be wondering why I recommend *War* after expressing my disapproval of ready-made sets in pictures such as Figure 9 (p. 37). I see a considerable difference between these activities. When the child decides, for example, whether or not 8 is greater than 9, he has to make a judgment that has immediate social consequences. When worksheets are used, this judgment is usually evaluated by the teacher much later. As stated in Principle 3(a), immediate feedback from peers is much better than deferred feedback from an adult.

I would like to conclude this discussion of group games with a problem that comes up in most games—the selection of "It" or of the first player. Most young children beg the teacher to give them this privileged role. The teacher has to be careful not to become the dispenser of this privilege. The best reaction in such a situation is to say, "I don't know whom to choose. How can *you* decide in a fair way?"

The most common solution is for one of the children to recite a rhyme, making each syllable correspond to one child in the order defined by the players' position in space. The player on whom the last syllable falls is the one chosen. When four-year-olds use this method, the rhyme sometimes goes faster than the hand, or vice versa. These children often end up designating themselves by not making a precise one-to-one correspondence. It often does not occur to the other four-year-olds in such a situation that there is something wrong with this procedure. Older children, who feel obliged to make a precise one-to-one correspondence, often figure out which person they must begin

---

[29]In first grade, some children decide to count the number of points, rather than the number of cards to determine the winner. Some children count by 5's to do this. Others put all the 1's together, all the 2's together, etc., and engage in a kind of multiplicatory thinking. That is, they count the total obtained with all the 1's, the total obtained with all the 2's, etc.

the rhyme with to make the last syllable fall on themselves. The thinking involved in this kind of attempt must be encouraged because intelligence develops by being used actively. If someone feels that this is cheating, the group can then deal with this problem.

If the children seem to be looking for an alternative way because the selected rhyme thus does not work any more, the teacher might suggest a different way of using chance. One way is to put as many chips as children in a bag, only one of which has a different color. The child who draws this one becomes the first player. Another way is to draw as many lines as children (see Figure 16), mark one of them with an "x" (Figure 16), and fold the paper to hide the "x" and the top ends of the lines. Each child then chooses one line and writes his name or initials at the bottom end. These ways of choosing the first player are much better for children's development of autonomy and numerical thinking than the adult's exercise of authority.

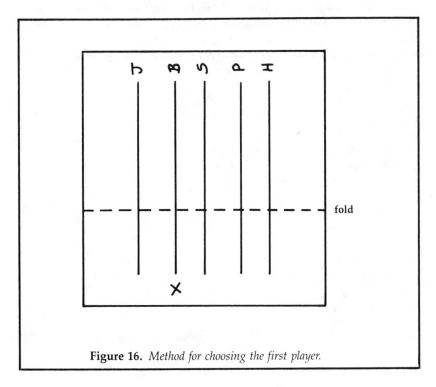

Figure 16. *Method for choosing the first player.*

In conclusion, I would like to return to the question posed at the beginning of this book: "Isn't there any way to apply the conservation task in the classroom?" My answer is that this task serves as an introduction to a far better theory of number than what we have had before, and as a springboard to further study. I tried in the above discussion to show that there are indirect and natural ways for the teacher to stimulate the creation of all kinds of relationships among all kinds of objects and events.

I also tried to show that there are ways of encouraging the quantification of objects within Piaget's framework, in ways that are far better than the lessons and exercises prescribed by most math educators. Educators unfamiliar with Piaget's theory may believe in the importance of the child's manipulating objects. However, they are stumped when asked *how* children learn number concepts by manipulating objects. Most answer the question by referring vaguely to empirical abstraction. The most original and fundamental idea in Piaget's theory of number is that of reflective abstraction and the child's construction of the numerical structure through reflective abstraction.

This book gave a few examples of activities tried in collaboration with a few teachers. I hope it will enable other teachers to go on to invent many others.

References

Adjei, K. "Influence of Specific Maternal Occupation and Behavior on Piagetian Cognitive Development." In *Piagetian Psychology: Cross-Cultural Contributions*, ed. P. Dasen. New York: Gardner Press, 1977.

Al-Fakhri, S. "The Conservation of Length in Children." Paper written at the Center of Psychological and Educational Research, University of Baghdad, 1973.

Al-Fakhri, S. "The Development of the Concept of Speed among Iraqi Children." In *Piagetian Psychology: Cross-Cultural Contributions*, ed. P. Dasen. New York: Gardner Press, 1977.

Al-Shaikh, A. A. "The Conservation of Length among Iraqi Children." Paper written at the University of Baghdad, 1974.

Almy, M. *Young Children's Thinking.* New York: Teachers College Press, 1966.

Almy, M. "The Usefulness of Piagetian Methods for Studying Primary School Children in Uganda." In *Studying School Children in Uganda*, ed. M. Almy, J. L. Duritz, and M. A. White. New York: Teachers College Press, 1970.

Bovet, M. C. "Cognitive Processes among Illiterate Children and Adults." In *Culture and Cognition: Readings in Cross-Cultural Psychology*, ed. J. W. Berry and P. R. Dasen. London: Methuen, 1974.

Capt, C.-L.; Glayre, L.; and Hegyi, A. *Des Activités de Connaissance Physique à l'Ecole Enfantine* (mémoire de licence, Université de Genève, 1976). Geneva: GRETI (Groupe de Réflexion et d'Etude sur l'Education et les Techniques d'Instruction), 1980.

Dasen, P. R. "Cross-Cultural Piagetian Research: A Summary." *Journal of Cross-Cultural Psychology* 3 (1972): 23–39.

Dasen, P. R. "The Influence of Ecology, Culture and European Contact on Cognitive Development in Australian Aborigines." In *Culture and Cognition: Readings in Cross-Cultural Psychology*, ed. J. W. Berry and P. R. Dasen. London: Methuen, 1974.

De Lacey, P. R. "A Cross-Cultural Study of Classificatory Ability in Australia." *Journal of Cross-Cultural Psychology* 1 (1970): 293–304.

De Lemos, M. M. "The Development of Conservation in Aboriginal Children." *International Journal of Psychology* 4 (1969): 255–269.

Duncan, E. R.; Capps, L. R.; Dolciani, M. P.; Quast, W. G.; and Zweng, M. J. *Modern School Mathematics: Structure and Use. Teacher's Annotated Ed.* Rev. ed. Boston: Houghton Mifflin, 1972.

Gillièron, C. "Serial Order and Vicariant Order: The Limits of Isomorphism." *Archives de Psychologie* 45 (1977): 183–204.

Gréco, P. "Quantité et Quotité." In *Structures Numériques Elémentaires* (Etudes d'Epistémologie Génétique, Vol. XIII), P. Gréco and A. Morf. Paris: Presses Universitaires de France, 1962.

Hyde, D. M. G. *Piaget and Conceptual Development.* London: Holt, Rinehart &

Winston, 1970.

Inhelder, B., and Piaget, J. *The Growth of Logical Thinking from Childhood to Adolescence.* New York: Basic Books, 1959 (first published in 1955).

Inhelder, B., and Piaget, J. *The Early Growth of Logic in the Child.* New York: Harper & Row, 1964 (first published in 1959).

Inhelder, B.; Sinclair, H.; and Bovet, M. *Learning and the Development of Cognition.* Cambridge, Mass.: Harvard University Press, 1974.

Kamii, C. "Application of Piaget's Theory to Education: The Pre-Operational Level." In *New Directions in Piagetian Theory and Practice,* ed. I. E. Sigel, D. M. Brodzinsky, and R. M. Golinkoff. Hillsdale, N.J.: Lawrence Erlbaum Associates, 1981.

Kamii, C., and DeVries, R. *Piaget, Children, and Number.* Washington, D.C.: National Association for the Education of Young Children, 1976.

Kamii, C., and DeVries, R. *Physical Knowledge in Preschool Education: Implications of Piaget's Theory.* Englewood Cliffs, N.J.: Prentice-Hall, 1978.

Kamii, C., and DeVries, R. *Group Games in Early Education: Implications of Piaget's Theory.* Washington, D.C.: National Association for the Education of Young Children, 1980.

Kunz, J. *Modern Mathematics Made Meaningful with Cuisenaire Rods.* New Rochelle, N.Y.: Cuisenaire Co. of America, 1965.

Laurendeau-Bendavid, M. "Culture, Schooling, and Cognitive Development: A Comparative Study of Children in French Canada and Rwanda." In *Piagetian Psychology: Cross-Cultural Contributions,* ed. P. Dasen. New York: Gardner Press, 1977.

Lavatelli, C. *Early Childhood Curriculum: A Piaget Program, Teacher's Guide.* 2nd ed. Boston: American Science and Engineering, 1973.

McKinnon, J. W., and Renner, J. W. "Are Colleges Concerned with Intellectual Development?" *American Journal of Physics* 39 (1971): 1047–1052.

Meljac, C. *Décrir, Agir et Compter.* Paris: Presses Universitaires de France, 1979.

Mohseni, N. "La Comparaison des Réactions aux Epreuves d'Intelligence en Iran et en Europe." Thesis, University of Paris, 1966.

Montessori, M. *The Montessori Method.* New York: Schocken, 1964 (first published in 1912).

Morf, A. "Recherches sur l'Origine de la Connexité de la Suite des Premiers Nombres." In *Structures Numériques Elémentaires* (Etudes d'Epistémologie Génétique, Vol. XIII), P. Gréco et A. Morf. Paris: Presses Universitaires de France, 1962.

Opper, S. "Concept Development in Thai Urban and Rural Children." In *Piagetian Psychology: Cross-Cultural Contributions,* ed. P. Dasen. New York: Gardner Press, 1977.

Perret-Clermont, A.-N. *Social Interaction and Cognitive Development in Children.* London: Academic Press, 1980.

Piaget, J. *The Child's Conception of the World.* Totowa, N.J.: Littlefield, Adams & Co., 1967 (first published in 1926).

Piaget, J. *The Moral Judgment of the Child.* New York: Free Press, 1965 (first published in 1932).

Piaget, J. *The Child's Conception of Time*. New York: Ballantine Books, 1971 (first published in 1946).

Piaget, J. *To Understand Is to Invent*. New York: Grossman, 1973 (first published in 1948).

Piaget, J. "Need and Significance of Cross-Cultural Studies in Genetic Psychology." *International Journal of Psychology* 1 (1966): 3–13.

Piaget, J. "Intellectual Evolution from Adolescence to Adulthood." *Human Development* 15 (1972): 1–12.

Piaget, J., and Garcia, R. *Understanding Causality*. New York: Norton, 1974 (first published in 1971).

Piaget, J., and Inhelder, B. *The Child's Construction of Quantities: Conservation and Atomism*. New York: Basic Books, 1974 (first published in 1941).

Piaget, J., and Inhelder, B. *The Child's Construction of Space*. New York: Norton, 1956 (first published in 1948).

Piaget, J., and Inhelder, B. *Mental Imagery in the Child*. London: Routledge & Kegan Paul, 1973 (first published in 1966).

Piaget, J.; Inhelder, B.; and Szeminska, A. *The Child's Conception of Geometry*. London: Routledge & Kegan Paul, 1952 (first published in 1948).

Piaget, J., and Szeminska, A. *The Child's Conception of Number*. London: Routledge & Kegan Paul, 1952 (first published in 1941).

Safar, S. "The Formation of the Concepts of Seriation and Serial Correspondences among Iraqi Children." Masters thesis, University of Baghdad, 1974.

Schwebel, M. "Formal Operations in First-Year College Students." *The Journal of Psychology* 91 (1975): 133–141.

Stern, C., and Stern, M.B. *Children Discover Arithmetic*. New York: Harper & Row, 1971.

Games

"Candy Land." Springfield, Mass.: Milton Bradley, 1955.

"Chutes and Ladders." Springfield, Mass.: Milton Bradley, 1956.

"Hi-Ho! Cherry-O." Racine, Wis.: Western Publishing, 1972.

"Piggy Bank." New York: Ed-U-Cards, 1965.

Appendix

Autonomy as the aim of education: *implications of Piaget's theory**

One of Piaget's books, *The Moral Judgment of the Child*, was published in 1932, and it is hard to believe that educators have not been influenced by this important book. In it, Piaget discussed the importance of the morality of autonomy. Autonomy means being governed by oneself. It is the opposite of heteronomy, which means being governed by someone else. An extreme example of the morality of autonomy can be seen in Elliott Richardson in the Watergate coverup affair. He was the only person under Nixon who refused to obey the boss and resigned from his position. The other people involved in the Watergate coverup illustrate the morality of heteronomy. When they were told to tell lies, they obeyed their superior and went along with what they knew to be wrong.

This Appendix is divided into three parts. In the first part, I continue to discuss the morality of autonomy. In the second part, I talk about the intellectual aspect of autonomy. In the third part, I conclude by discussing more specifically autonomy as the aim of education.

Moral autonomy

Piaget gave commonplace examples of the morality of autonomy. In

*Keynote address given at the annual conference of the North Carolina Association for the Education of Young Children, Winston-Salem, October 16, 1981, and at the annual conference of the DuPage Regional Unit of the Chicago Association for the Education of Young Children, Glen Ellyn, Illinois, October 17, 1981.

his research, he asked children between the ages of 6 and 14 whether it was worse to tell a lie to an adult or to another child. Young children consistently replied that it was worse to tell a lie to an adult. When asked why, they explained that adults can tell when a statement is not true. Older children, in contrast, tended to answer that sometimes one almost has to lie to adults, but it is rotten to do it to other children. This is an example of the morality of autonomy. For autonomous people, lies are bad independently of whether one is caught or not.

Piaget made up many pairs of stories and asked children which one of the two children was the worse. Following is an example of such a pair:

> A little boy (or a little girl) goes for a walk in the street and meets a big dog who frightens him very much. So then he goes home and tells his mother he has seen a dog that was as big as a cow.

> A child comes home from school and tells his mother that the teacher had given him good marks, but it was not true; the teacher had given him no marks at all, either good or bad. Then his mother was very pleased and rewarded him. (1932, p. 148)

Young children systematically manifested the morality of heteronomy by saying that it was worse to say "I saw a dog as big as a cow." Why was it worse? Because dogs are never as big as cows and adults do not believe such stories. Older, more autonomous children, however, tended to say that it was worse to say "The teacher gave me good marks" *because* this lie is more believable.

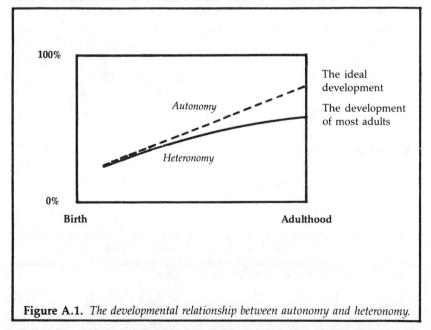

Figure A.1. *The developmental relationship between autonomy and heteronomy.*

Figure A.1 shows the developmental relationship between autonomy and heteronomy. In this figure, time is represented along the horizontal axis from birth to adulthood. The vertical axis represents the proportion of autonomy in relation to heteronomy, from 0 to 100 percent. The dotted line shows the ideal development of an individual. All babies are born helpless and heteronomous. Ideally, the child becomes increasingly more autonomous as he grows older, and as he becomes more autonomous, he becomes less heteronomous. In other words, to the extent that the child becomes able to govern himself, he is governed less by other people.

In reality, most adults did not develop in this ideal way. The great majority stopped developing at a low level as shown by the solid line in Figure A.1. Piaget (1948) said that it is a rare adult who is truly moral. This observation can easily be confirmed in our daily life. Newspapers are full of stories about corruption in government and about theft, assault, and murder.

What makes some adults morally autonomous?

The important question for educators and parents is what causes some children to become morally autonomous adults. Piaget's answer to this question was that adults reinforce children's natural heteronomy when they use reward and punishment, and they stimulate the development of autonomy when they exchange points of view with children.

When a child tells a lie, for example, the adult can deprive him of dessert or make him write 50 times "I will not lie." The adult can also refrain from punishing the child and, instead, look him straight in the eye with great skepticism and affection and say, "I really can't believe what you are saying because . . . . " This is an example of an exchange of points of view that contributes to the development of autonomy in children. The child who can see that the adult cannot believe him can be motivated to think about what he must do to be believed. The child who is raised with many similar opportunities can, over time, construct for himself the conviction that it is best eventually for people to deal honestly with each other.

Punishment leads to three possible outcomes. The most common one is calculation of risks. The child who is punished will repeat the same act but try to avoid being caught the next time. Adults can sometimes even be heard saying, "Don't let me catch you doing that again!" Sometimes, the child stoically decides ahead of time that even if he is caught, the price will be worth paying for the pleasure he will have. The second possible outcome of punishment is blind conformity. Some compliant children become perfect conformists because conformity assures them of security and respectability. When they become complete conformists, children do not have to make decisions any more, as all they have to do is obey. The third possible outcome is revolt. Some children behave very well for years but decide at a certain point that they are tired of pleasing their parents and teachers all the time, and that the time has come for them to begin living for themselves. They may thus even begin to engage in various behaviors that characterize delinquency. These behaviors may look like autonomous acts, but there is a vast difference between autonomy and revolt. In a revolt, the person is against conformity, but nonconformity does not necessarily make a person morally autonomous.

Punishment thus reinforces children's heteronomy and prevents them from developing autonomy. While rewards are nicer than punishments, they, too, reinforce children's heteronomy. Children who help parents only to get money, and those who study only to get good marks are governed by others, just like children who are "good" only to avoid being punished. Adults exercise power over children by using rewards and punishments, and it is these sanctions that keep children obedient and heteronomous.

If we want children to develop the morality of autonomy, we must reduce our adult power by refraining from using rewards and punishments, and encourage them to construct for themselves their own moral values. For example, the child has the possibility of thinking about the importance of honesty only if he is not punished for telling lies and is, instead, confronted with the fact that other people cannot believe or trust him.

The essence of autonomy is that children become able to make decisions for themselves. Autonomy is not the same thing as complete freedom. Autonomy means taking relevant factors into account in deciding what the best course of action might be for all concerned. There can be no morality when one considers only one's own point of view. If one takes other people's point of view into account, one is not free to tell lies, break promises, and be inconsiderate.

Piaget was realistic enough to say that in the reality of life, it is impossible to avoid punishments. Streets are full of cars, and we obviously cannot allow children to touch stereo sets and electric outlets. Piaget, however, made an important distinction between punishment and sanctions by reciprocity. Depriving the child of dessert for telling a lie is an example of a punishment, as the relationship between a lie and dessert is completely arbitrary. Telling him that we cannot believe what he said is an example of a sanction by reciprocity. Sanctions by reciprocity are directly related to the act we want to sanction and to the adult's point of view, and have the effect of motivating the child to construct rules of conduct for himself, through the coordination of viewpoints.

Piaget (1932, Chapter 3) gave six examples of sanctions by reciprocity. I would like to relate four of the six examples. The first one is temporary or permanent exclusion from the group. When a child disturbs adults at the dinner table, parents often say, "You can either stay here without bothering us or go to your room and be noisy." This sanction is related to the act sanctioned and to the adults' point of view, and gives to the child the possibility of constructing for himself the rule of being considerate to other people. To be sure, the choice offered is coercive and between two things he dislikes, but the important element is the possibility of making a decision. The implication here is that when and if he decides to be quiet, he has the possibility of coming back to the group.

Teachers often use this sanction of exclusion from the group. When a group is listening to a story and a child disrupts the group, for example, the teacher often says, "You can either stay here without bothering the rest of us, or I must ask you to go to the book corner and read by yourself." Whenever possible, the child must be given the possibility of deciding when he can behave well enough to return to the group. Mechanical time limits serve only as punishment, and children who have served the required time often feel perfectly free to commit the same misdeed again.

The second type of sanction by reciprocity is appeal to the direct and material consequence of the act. I have already given an example of this type of sanction in connection with children's lies.

The third type of sanction by reciprocity is depriving the child of the thing he has misused. Some time ago, I was in a classroom of four- and five-year-olds for three days in succession. The room was rather small for a class of about 25 children, and about one-third of its surface was set aside for block constructions that stayed up throughout my visit. I was surprised that the elaborate constructions stayed up for three days and that the children were extremely careful not to disturb anybody else's work when they went to the block area from time to time to modify their products. When I asked the teacher how she got the children to be so careful, she explained that she was very strict at the beginning of the year and did not let children go in the block area if they knocked anything over. Later, she said, she negotiated with individual children the right to go in that area when they knew that this right had to be earned.

The fourth type of sanction by reciprocity is restitution. For example, if a young child spills paint on the floor, an appropriate reaction may be to say, "Would you like me to help you clean it up?" Later in the year, it may be enough just to ask, "What do you have to do?"

One day, in a kindergarten class, a child came up to the teacher crying because his art project had been damaged. The teacher turned to the class and said that she wanted the person who broke the object to stay with her during recess so that she could help him repair the object. The child responsible for the breakage could see the point of view of the victim, and was encouraged to construct for himself the rule of restitution. When children are not afraid of being punished, they are perfectly willing to come forward and make restitution. The teacher helped the child repair the broken object and told him that next time something similar happens, she wanted him to tell her so that she could help him fix the object again.

Piaget pointed out that all the preceding sanctions can quickly degenerate into punishments if there is no relationship of mutual affection and respect between the adult and the child. Mutual respect is, in fact, essential for the child's development of autonomy. The child who feels respected for the way he thinks and feels is likely to feel respect for the way adults think and feel.

Constructivism

Piaget's theory about how children learn moral values is fundamentally different from other, traditional theories and from common sense. In the traditional view, the child is believed to acquire moral values by internalizing them from the environment. According to Piaget, children acquire moral values not by internalizing or absorbing them from the environment but by constructing them from the inside, through interaction with the environment. For example, no child is taught that it is worse to tell a lie to an adult than to another child. Yet young children construct this belief out of what they have been told. Likewise, no child is taught that it is worse to say, "I saw a dog as big as a cow" than to say, "The teacher gave me good marks." But young children make such judgments by putting into relationship everything they have been told. Fortunately, they go on to construct other relationships and many of them end up believing that it is worse to say "The teacher gave me good marks."

It is probably safe to say that all of us have been punished when we were children. To the extent that we also had the possibility of coordinating viewpoints with others, we had the possibility of becoming more autonomous. Elliott Richardson was probably raised to make decisions by considering other people's points of view, rather than by considering only the reward system.

The Watergate affair illustrates Piaget's view that autonomy is not only moral but also intellectual. The men who ended up going to prison were, of course, immoral, but they can also be said to have been unbelievably stupid, like young children who are too egocentric to know that the truth will be revealed sooner or later anyway. I would now like to examine the child's development of intellectual autonomy.

Intellectual autonomy

In the intellectual realm, too, autonomy means self-governing, and heteronomy means being governed by somebody else. An extreme example of intellectual autonomy is Copernicus, or the inventor of any other revolutionary theory in the history of science. Copernicus invented the heliocentric theory when everybody else believed that the sun went around the earth. He was even laughed off the stage, but was autonomous enough to remain convinced of his own idea. An intellectually heteronomous person, by contrast, unquestioningly believes what he is told, including illogical conclusions, slogans, and propaganda.

A more common example of intellectual autonomy is my niece, who used to believe in Santa Claus. When she was about six, she surprised her mother one day by asking, "How come Santa Claus uses the same wrapping paper as we do?" Her mother's "explanation" satisfied her for a few minutes, but she soon came up with the next question: "How come Santa Claus has the same handwriting as Daddy?" This child had her own way of thinking, which was different from what she had been taught.

According to Piaget, the child acquires knowledge by constructing it from within, rather than by internalizing it directly from the environment. Children may internalize the knowledge taught for a while, but they are not passive vessels that merely hold what is poured into their heads. A more precise way of discussing constructivism is to say that children construct knowledge by creating and coordinating relationships. When my niece put Santa Claus into relationship with everything else she knew, she began to feel that something was wrong somewhere. Since the presents she received from outside the family usually came in different wraps, she became suspicious of those that came in the familiar paper. It is true that people can buy the same kind of paper in stores, but when children are not convinced by what they are told, they rack their brains to make sense of the situation.

Unfortunately, in school, children are not encouraged to think autonomously. Teachers use sanctions in the intellectual realm, too, to get children to give the "right" answers they want to hear. An example of this practice is the use of worksheets. In first grade arithmetic, for example, if a child writes "$4 + 2 = 5$," most teachers mark it as being wrong. The result of this kind of teaching is that children become convinced that truth can come only out of the teacher's head. Furthermore, when I walk around a first grade classroom while children are working on arithmetic worksheets, and stop to ask individual children how they got particular answers, they typically react by grabbing their erasers and erasing like mad, even when their answer is perfectly correct! Already in first grade, many children have learned to distrust their own thinking. Children who are thus discouraged from thinking autonomously will construct less knowledge than those who are mentally active and confident.

If a child says that $4 + 2 = 5$, the best reaction is to refrain from correcting him and ask him instead, "How did you get 5?" Children often correct themselves autonomously as they try to explain their reasoning to someone else. The child who tries to explain his reasoning has to decenter to make sense to the other person. While thus trying to coordinate his point of view with another viewpoint, the child often realizes his own mistake.

An even better way of teaching arithmetic in first grade is by eliminating all instruction and introducing many games such as *Double War*. This game is played like *War*, except that the sum of two cards is compared with the sum of the opponent's cards as shown in Figure A.2. Children do not need to be taught sums because they can figure out for themselves the result of each addition. In a game, furthermore, they can exchange points of view with other players when one says, for example, that $2 + 4 = 5$. This way of learning is much more active and conducive to the development of autonomy than worksheets. In my current research, I find that children cannot help remembering sums if they play these games often enough.

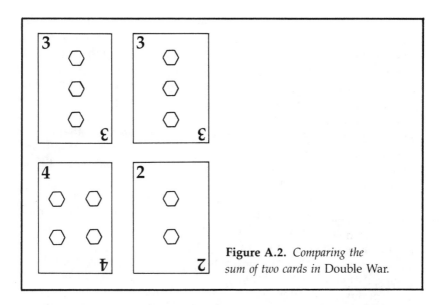

Figure A.2. *Comparing the sum of two cards in* Double War.

The coordination of points of view among peers is more effective, according to Piaget's constructivism, than correction by the teacher. Following is an example of the teaching of grammar in a sixth grade class.

The class was learning to diagram sentences, and the group was divided into six subgroups of four or five pupils each. When I arrived after lunch, the teacher put a rather tricky sentence on the board and gave the groups 20 minutes to diagram it. When the time was up, a representative of each group went to the board and put a diagram on it. Two of the six diagrams were immediately erased, as they duplicated two other groups'. Individual students then offered well-reasoned arguments in favor of one diagram, or to show that one was inadequate. The author of the version under attack would then defend it vigorously. The arguments thus continued with intensity until it was time for recess. By that time, everybody had agreed that two of the four versions could not be defended and had to be erased.

When the children returned from recess, the teacher asked if the class wanted the answer. Some said "Yes," but others answered, "No, because you'll give us the wrong answer just to see if you can trick us!" The teacher admitted that he indeed intended to do that. The arguments and counterarguments continued, and the class finally agreed on the superiority of one diagram.

This class spent an entire afternoon on one sentence. But I was left with the impression that the children thought so hard about each well-articulated idea that they were thoroughly convinced of the superiority of the final diagram. Many children offered wrong ideas along the way, but they were encouraged to defend their opinion until they were convinced that they were wrong. Children learn by modifying old ideas, according to constructivism, rather than by accumulating new bits. A debate about the superiority of one diagram or another is good because it encourages children to put different opinions critically into relationship, and to modify old ideas when they are convinced that a new idea is better.

Teachers at all age levels including the university can teach in ways similar to the sixth grade teacher above that encourage the learner's intellectual autonomy. Unfortunately in school, students are made to recite "right" answers, and are seldom asked what they honestly think.

Educators in early education often define their objectives today by saying that children must learn so-called "concepts," such as the concepts of numbers, letters, colors, geometric shapes, *over, under, between, left to right, long, longer, and longest, first, second, and third*, etc. I am opposed to this way of defining objectives because it directs the teacher to teach one unrelated word after another, rather than encouraging children to construct knowledge in relation to what they already know. This way of imposing lists of words is like trying to grow a tree by pasting leaves from the outside. Leaves grow out of the plant, from within, and every plant and animal develops from within, with its own organization.

Another contemporary preoccupation is with what is called "minimum competencies" necessary for the child to be allowed to go on to the next grade. The minimum competency necessary in arithmetic for first graders where I am currently doing research is having memorized sums to ten. The children in the regular first grade class had worksheets and daily drill to memorize these sums. The children I worked with, however, had no instruction, no drill, no worksheet, and no pressure. They only played games such as *Double War*. The comparison of the results can be seen in Tables A.1 and A.2.

The moral of this story for me is that if you require minimum competencies, you will only get minimum competencies! Children who are encouraged to think actively, critically, and autonomously learn more than those who are made to have minimum competencies.

Having discussed what Piaget meant by moral and intellectual autonomy, I would now like to discuss more specifically autonomy as the aim of education.

	Experimental $N=24$	Control $N=12$	Difference
2 + 2	100	100	0
5 + 5	100	92	8
3 + 3	100	100	0
4 + 1	100	100	0
6 + 1	100	100	0
5 + 1	100	100	0
1 + 4	100	100	0
2 + 3	100	92	8
5 + 2	100	92	8
4 + 4	96	100	–4
1 + 5	96	100	–4
6 + 6	88	75	13
4 + 2	88	83	5
3 + 2	88	92	–4
2 + 5	88	92	–4
6 + 2	88	83	5
2 + 6	88	67	21
6 + 3	79	67	12
4 + 5	75	92	–17
2 + 4	75	92	–17
5 + 4	71	83	–12
4 + 3	71	83	–12
3 + 4	71	75	–4
4 + 6	67	50	17
5 + 3	63	83	–20
3 + 6	63	67	–3
3 + 5	63	75	–12
6 + 5	54	58	–4
5 + 6	50	58	–8

Table A. 1. Percent of first graders who gave the correct answer immediately: addends up to six. June 1981.

Autonomy as the aim of education

Figure A.3 shows autonomy as the aim of education in relation to the goals of education defined today by most educators and the public. The shaded part of the circle to the right (labeled "the goals of most educators and the public") that does not overlap with the other circle stands for things we memorized in school just to pass one examination after another. All of us who succeeded in school achieved this success

	Experimental N=24	Control N=12	Difference
9 + 1	100	100	0
7 + 2	100	83	17
1 + 10	100	92	8
10 + 10	100	75	25
2 + 8	88	67	21
7 + 3	83	67	16
9 + 2	79	67	12
9 + 9	63	58	5
8 + 5	54	42	12
8 + 8	54	42	12
7 + 7	50	50	0
5 + 7	50	58	–8
7 + 8	38	25	13

Table A. 2. Percent of first graders who gave the correct answer immediately: addends seven to ten. June 1981.

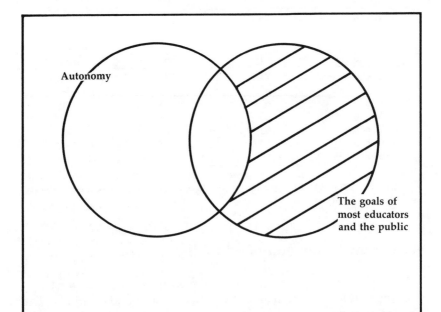

Figure A.3. *Autonomy as the aim of education in relation to the goals of education learned today by most educators and the public.*

by memorizing an enormous number of words without understanding them or caring about them. All of us remember the joy of being free to forget the things we memorized only to pass a test. We made these efforts mostly because we were good, obedient conformists.

The result of this kind of education is what McKinnon and Renner (1971) and Schwebel (1975) found in their research on college freshmen's ability to think logically at the formal operational level. These college students were the outstanding ones in elementary and secondary schools who were successful enough to enter the university. The percentage found by McKinnon and Renner to be capable of solid logical thinking at the formal level was 25. The percent found by Schwebel was only 20.

Ability to think logically at the formal level belongs to the circle labeled "autonomy" in Figure A.3. More precisely, it belongs to the part of the circle that does not overlap with the other circle, since so few college freshmen seem to have formal operations after being successful in secondary school. After presenting their findings, McKinnon and Renner asked what kind of education these university students received in high school. They concluded that high schools do not teach students to think logically, and that if high school teachers do not emphasize logical thinking, we must ask who trained these teachers. Their answer was: Universities did. In other words, schools underemphasize thinking from beginning to end. If students cannot think logically at the formal-operational level, they certainly cannot think critically or autonomously.

In the moral realm, too, as I stated earlier, today's schools reinforce children's heteronomy and unwittingly prevent them from developing autonomy. To enforce adults' rules and standards, schools use tests, grades, gold stars, the detention hall, merits and demerits, and awards. The part of the circle labeled "autonomy" that does not overlap with the other circle thus stands for intellectual and moral autonomy.

The intersection between the two circles stands for things we learned in school that were useful to our development of autonomy. The ability to read and write, to do arithmetic, to read maps and charts, and to situate events in history are examples of what we learned in school that is useful for our adaptation to the environment. *If autonomy is the aim of education, attempts must be made to increase the area of overlap between the two circles.*

In conclusion, Piaget's theory does not imply the invention of just another method to get to the same, traditional goals. Autonomy as the aim of education implies a new conceptualization of objectives. I do not have anything against correct answers or the 3 R's. In fact, I support them. But there is an enormous difference between a correct answer produced autonomously with personal conviction and one produced heteronomously by obedience. There is likewise an enormous difference between "good" behavior autonomously chosen and "good" behavior through blind conformity.

Ironically, many educators would like to see the morality of autonomy and intellectual autonomy in their pupils. The tragedy is that, because they do not know the distinction between autonomy and heteronomy, and because they have outdated ideas about what makes children "good" and "educated," they continue to depend on rewards and punishments, convinced that these are essential for producing good, intelligent future adult citizens.

Education is an underdeveloped profession that is now at a level similar to the pre-Copernican stage of astronomy. Just as astronomers before Copernicus made many small corrections for specific predictions about planets' positions that did not work, educators are trying to solve a variety of problems such as low test scores, apathy, truancy, drug abuse, and vandalism as if these were separate problems. Piaget's theory of autonomy suggests the need for a Copernican revolution in education. By shifting the focus of our thinking from what *we* do to how *children* develop, we can begin to view academic subjects and moral education from the standpoint of how children learn.

What education needs more than money today is a fundamental reconceptualization of objectives. By focusing on the child's autonomy, we may well foster development of children with old values, such as love of learning and self-discipline. Children respect the rules *they* make for themselves. They also work hard to achieve the goals *they* set for themselves. Autonomy as the aim of education is in a sense a new idea that will revolutionize education. In another sense, however, it can be viewed as a return to old human values and human relationships.

Appendix references

McKinnon, J. W., and Renner, J. W. "Are Colleges Concerned with Intellectual Development?" *American Journal of Physics* 39 (1971): 1047–1052.

Piaget, J. *The Moral Judgment of the Child.* New York: Free Press, 1965 (first published in 1932).

Piaget, J. *To Understand Is to Invent.* New York: Viking, 1973 (first published in 1948).

Schwebel, M. "Formal Operations in First-Year College Students." *The Journal of Psychology* 91 (1975): 133–141.

Index

Information about NAEYC

NAEYC is . . .

. . . a membership organization of people committed to fostering the growth and development of children from birth through age eight. Membership is open to all who share a desire to serve and act on behalf of the needs and rights of young children.

NAEYC provides . . .

. . . educational services and resources to adults who work with and for children, including
- *Young Children,* the *journal* for early childhood educators
- **Books, posters, and brochures** to expand your knowledge and commitment to young children with topics including infants, curriculum, research, discipline, teacher education, and parent involvement
- An **Annual Conference** that brings people from all over the country to share their expertise and advocate on behalf of children and families
- **Week of the Young Child** celebrations sponsored by NAEYC Affiliate Groups across the country to call public attention to the needs and rights of children and families
- **Insurance plans** for individuals and programs
- **Public policy information** for informed advocacy efforts at all levels of government
- The **National Academy of Early Childhood Programs,** a voluntary accreditation system for high quality programs for young children
- The **Information Service,** a computer-based, centralized source of information sharing, distribution, and collaboration

For free information about membership, publications, or other NAEYC services. . .

. . . Call NAEYC at 202-232-8777 or 800-424-2460
or write to **NAEYC**
> **1834 Connecticut Avenue, N.W.**
> **Washington, DC 20009-5786**